NEW PRACTICE READERS

THIRD EDITION

BOOK D

DONALD G. ANDERSON

Associate Superintendent, Retired
Oakland Public Schools
Oakland, California

CLARENCE R. STONE
with ANNE ELIASBERG

Phoenix Learning Resources
New York • St. Louis

NEW PRACTICE READERS
THIRD EDITION
BOOK D

Project Management and Production: Kane Publishing Services, Inc.
Cover Design: Pencil Point Studios
Text Design: Craven and Evans, Inc.

ISBN 0-7915-2120-6

  5 6 7 8 9

TO THE TEACHER

This book is one of a seven-book series. It is intended to provide reading interest along with the development of comprehension skills for readers who need additional practice material to achieve mastery. The controlled reading level of each book makes it possible to assign students to the text most suitable for individual reading comfort.

Readabilities for this book are 4.4–5.5, consistent with the Dale-Chall Readability Formula. The reading level should be comfortable for students whose reading skills are adequate for beginning fifth grade according to standardized tests.

This book contains nine groups of articles in units labeled A–I. The subjects cover the major content fields listed below.

1. Animals and reptiles
2. Faraway places
3. Insects
4. Geography
5. Foods
6. Explaining nature
7. Measures and mathematical aids
8. History and legend
9. Biography

Before each reading selection, there is a readiness activity to introduce difficult words. Teacher supervision at this point will be helpful to later success.

Following the factual articles are tests designed to improve specific skills for study reading. Charts at the end of each book provide a place for individual records of progress on each skill.

The six basic skills tested are consistent with those that appear on widely accepted reading achievement tests. In Book D they are:

1. Implied details. The answer here must be selected from among a group of possibilities. The correct answer is a reasonable conclusion (not one stated in the article) from ideas contained in the reading material. Answering and discussing such questions will give students valuable experience in reasoning.

2. Meaning of the whole. These questions require that students select the answer that best describes the central theme of the article.

3. Recognition of antecedents. Students must show that they know which word or group of words is referred to by such common pronouns as **they, some, it, who, those, this,** and **each**.

4. Determining whether a given idea has been stated affirmatively, negatively, or not at all within the reading matter. This question requires a recognition of the difference between assumptions, however reasonable, and evidence.

5. Awareness of the falseness of a statement in relation to the selection.

6. Recognition of the meaning of a word in context.

At the conclusion of each unit of nine articles there is a longer story prepared for recreational reading. Many of these stories come from folktales and are intended as pleasure reading and as a basis for group discussion. The *Thinking It Over* questions following each story may be used to launch the discussion. In certain cases, students may be requested to write answers comprised of whole sentences in order to develop additional skills.

All of the selections may be used with average or better readers to develop reading speed when desired. Students should be urged to increase their speed only in terms of their individual results.

A sample exercise precedes the regular lessons. Directions explain the procedure. Ideally, the teacher will work through the sample exercise with the entire group.

Read-along cassettes to help the most dependent students are available for Books A, B, C, and D.

TABLE OF CONTENTS

HOW TO USE THIS BOOK

There are three parts to each lesson.
1. Questions to help you get ready.
Read them. Write the answers.

Getting Ready to Read

SAY AND KNOW

voyage
warrior
measure
single
village
settle
settlements
establish
consider
important
discovery

Draw a line under each right answer or fill in the blank.

1. It means **one**.   **single**   **important**   **village**

2. **To set up** means to   **remember**   **discover**   **establish**.

3. **An ocean trip** is a   **settlement**   **discovery**   **voyage**.

4. **A fighter** is a   **warrior**   **settlement**   **voyage**.

5. **To think about** is to   **settle**   **consider**   **measure**.

6. **To find length and width** is to _____.

---

2. A story to read.

Sample   Brave Sailors

Several hundred years before the voyages of Columbus, America was visited by people called Vikings. These brave warriors came from Norway, Sweden, Denmark, and Iceland. Many of them were good sailors and made long voyages. They learned to make strong boats that could travel long distances over the seas. These were small ships. They measured about 21 meters (70 feet) long and 5 meters (16 feet) wide. They had oars and single sails.

In many countries, the Vikings were feared. Sweeping down upon towns and villages, they would loot and burn them. Then they would return to their ships. Sometimes, however, the Vikings would settle in a place. Then they would quickly learn the ways of the people.

There are signs that the Vikings established small settlements in North America. These settlements, however, did not last, so the visits of the Vikings to the New World were not considered as important as those of later explorers. Even so, these brave people played a part in the discovery of America.

3. Questions to tell how well you read.
   Read them.   Write the answers.
   Put the number you get right in the box.

Sample   Testing Yourself

NUMBER RIGHT

Draw a line under each right answer or fill in each blank.

1. Although not stated in the article, you can tell that
      a. Vikings invented boats.   b. Vikings were sometimes farmers.
            c. Vikings were at home at sea.

2. This article as a whole is about
      a. ancient fishers.   c. Vikings.
      b. discovering America.   d. early settlements.

3. The word **they** in the second paragraph, second sentence, refers to

                              _____.

4. Viking ships had sails.   Yes   No   Does not say

5. Which two of these sentences are not true?
      a. Vikings were never peaceful.   c. Vikings were feared.
      b. Columbus was a Viking.   d. Vikings were brave.
         e. Vikings may have had settlements in North America.

6. What word in the first sentence means **sea trips?** _____

1

Answers for the Sample

Check your work. If you made a mistake, find out why. Count your number right and mark the score on your paper.

Getting Ready	Testing Yourself
1. single	1. c
2. establish	2. c
3. voyage	3. Vikings
4. warrior	4. Yes
5. consider	5. a, b
6. measure	6. voyages

Keeping Track of Your Progress

At the back of this book, on page 186, there are record charts. Turn to the charts and read the directions. After you finish each lesson, record your score. Keep track of how you are doing on each type of question.

If you may not mark in this book, make a copy of the charts for your notebook.

NEW PRACTICE READERS

THIRD EDITION

BOOK D

Getting Ready to Read

member
llama
moisture
stubborn
refuse
angry
nomads
saliva
beast
burden
young

Draw a line under each right answer or fill in the blank.

1. It means **wetness.**   burden   saliva   moisture

2. **The opposite of old** is   stubborn   young   angry.

3. **A load** is a   llama   member   burden.

4. **The opposite of accept** is   refuse   beast   angry.

5. It is **the name of one animal.**   llama   stubborn   nomad

6. **One who belongs to a group** is called a

_____.

A-1   Mountain Camels

Llamas are members of the camel family. They live in large flocks in the Andes Mountains of South America. A full-grown llama measures about 4 feet (a little over a meter) tall at the shoulder. However, it can easily carry a load of about 100 pounds (45 kilograms). Llamas can climb well. They can live on the plants that grow high up the mountains. In addition, llamas can go for days without water. They get moisture from green plants.

Llamas can be very stubborn. A tired llama or one that has too big a load may lie down and refuse to

move. When a llama is angry or afraid, it will spit bad-smelling saliva. Sometimes it may even throw up.

Llamas are used as beasts of burden by the people living in the Andes Mountains. In addition, these people use llama hair to make warm cloth and llama hide to make shoes. Sometimes they even use young llamas for food. As you can see, llamas are as useful to the mountain people as camels are to the nomads of the desert.

A-1   Testing Yourself

NUMBER RIGHT

Draw a line under each right answer or fill in each blank.

1. Although not stated in the article, you can tell that
  a. llamas make good pets.   b. llamas are similar to camels.
  c. llamas look like cats.

2. This article as a whole is about
  a. the Andes Mountains.   c. llamas and their uses.
  b. mountain travel.   d. South America.

3. The word **one** in the second paragraph, second sentence, refers to

_____.

4. Llamas have humps.   Yes   No   Does not say

5. Which two of these sentences are not true?
  a. Llamas sometimes spit.   c. Llamas are not strong.
  b. Indians eat llamas.   d. Llamas live in flocks.
      e. Llamas need water three times each day.

6. What word in the last sentence means **wanderers?** _____

Getting Ready to Read

SAY AND KNOW

Tokyo
capital
Japan
subways
airport
high rise
television
Kyoto
modern
tasty
sauces

Draw a line under each right answer or fill in the blank.

1. Subways   **are like taxis**   **run below ground**   **are high rise.**

2. A high-rise building is always   **tall**   **modern**   **old.**

3. It is **something to eat.**   **sauce**   **capital**   **television**

4. Plays are given in   **a theater**   **a subway**   **an airport.**

5. **The opposite of old-fashioned** is   **modern**   **high**   **beautiful.**

6. Food that tastes good is _____.

A-2   Anyone for Tokyo?

Tokyo is the capital city of Japan. It is one of the three largest cities in the world. In some ways, Tokyo is like New York or other big American cities. Its streets are crowded with people, cars, trucks, buses, and taxis. It has fast trains and subways. It has a large airport, high-rise hotels, big stores, and a tall television tower. And baseball is a favorite sport in Tokyo.

For over 200 years, Tokyo has been the capital of Japan. But hundreds of years ago, Japan's capital was an inland city named Kyoto. Unlike many places in Japan, the lovely city of Kyoto was not harmed in World War II. Visitors today can see the old city looking much the same as it did long ago. It remains a city of the past while the modern capital Tokyo keeps changing.

Many things in Tokyo, however, are old and native to Japan. If you went there, you would see the beautiful Imperial Palace. You might visit a theater to see actors present Japanese folktales. You might try a dish the Japanese like. One special dish is made of slices of raw fish served with tasty sauces. And then again, you might join many young Japanese and go to a baseball game. Anyone for Tokyo?

A-2 Testing Yourself

NUMBER RIGHT

Draw a line under each right answer or fill in each blank.

1. Although not stated in the article, you can tell that
   a. Tokyo is a large city.
   b. Tokyo has traffic problems.
   c. Tokyo became the capital about 200 years ago.

2. This article as a whole is about
   a. Japanese food.
   b. people in Tokyo.
   c. the capital of Japan.
   d. the city of Kyoto.

3. The word **its** in the first paragraph, fourth sentence, refers to _____

4. Tokyo is not a crowded city.   Yes   No   Does not say

5. Which two of these sentences are not true?
   a. Tokyo is Japan's capital.
   b. Tokyo has no trains or subways.
   c. Tokyo has new buildings.
   d. The Imperial Palace is in Tokyo.
   e. Tokyo has been the capital for many hundreds of years.

6. What word in the last paragraph, fifth sentence means **things that are served with raw fish**? _____

Getting Ready to Read

SAY AND KNOW

leaves
distance
trail
form
press
substance
mushroom
similar
furnish
producing
grower

Draw a line under each right answer or fill in the blank.

1. It means **provide.**   furnish   form   press

2. **The space between** is the   trail   press   distance.

3. **Shape** means   substance   mushroom   form.

4. They are **part of a plant.**   trail   similar   leaves

5. It means **somewhat alike.**   similar   form   grower

6. **Making** means _____.

A-3   Mushroom-Growers

Certain ants in Central and South America make and use small roads to go from one place to another. These ants are called leaf-cutting ants. They may travel long distances from their homes to find trees. From these trees, they cut small pieces of leaves. Carrying the pieces of leaves in their mouths, the ants go back to their nests. They use the same trails they have made.

After taking its piece of leaf down into the nest, each ant forms

it into a little ball. The ant does not eat the balls it makes. It presses them against the inside of the nest until a sort of garden is made. The balls of leaves form a wall.

The queen ant then adds a substance to the garden. The substance causes a plant similar to the mushroom to grow. When this plant has grown, the ants eat it. The plant furnishes most of their food supply. Because of their way of producing food, leaf-cutting ants are also called "mushroom-growers."

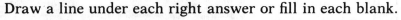

A-3   Testing Yourself

NUMBER RIGHT

Draw a line under each right answer or fill in each blank.

1. Although not stated in the article, you can tell that
  a. these ants eat leaves.   b. these ants live in hives.
     c. the queen ant is different from the other ants.

2. This article as a whole is about
  a. growing mushrooms.   c. ants producing food.
  b. making a leaf garden.   d. different mushrooms.

3. The word **them** in the second paragraph, third sentence, refers to

_____.

4. Leaf-cutting ants eat leaves.   Yes   No   Does not say

5. Which two of these sentences are not true?
  a. These ants live in South America.   c. These ants eat their queen.
  b. These ants have a queen.   d. Some ants make food.
     e. Leaf-cutting ants eat only things they grow.

6. What word in the first sentence means **one kind?** _____

9

Getting Ready to Read

Draw a line under each right answer or fill in the blank.

1. It means **to be without.** station protect lack

2. **Going from one place to another** is traveling ship space.

3. **The opposite of nighttime** is space daytime mineral.

4. **Coal** is **a mineral** **an astronaut** **a station.**

5. **Boats** are **parts** **ships** travels.

6. **Very cold** means _____ cold.

A-4 Neighbor in the Sky

The moon is much smaller than the sun and the stars. But to us, it seems larger. It looks larger because it is closer to Earth than any stars or planet. The moon is close enough so that astronauts traveling in space ships have visited it.

The air around the Earth protects it from the sun's rays. Air also keeps the Earth from losing too much heat. The moon grows extremely hot in the daytime and extremely cold at night. That happens because the moon has no air blanket to protect it.

The astronauts who went to the moon brought back pieces of moon rock and moon soil. New minerals were found in the moon

rocks. But moon rocks lacked other things found in earth rock.

Lack of air and water seems to make moon life impossible. But our space travelers set up stations on the moon that can radio messages to Earth. In this way, we are always learning new facts about the moon.

Do you think that you will ever spend a vacation on the moon?

A-4   Testing Yourself

NUMBER RIGHT

Draw a line under each right answer or fill in each blank.

1. Although not stated in the article, you can tell that
    a. distant things seem large.   b. more distant things seem smaller.
    c. all stars are smaller than our moon.

2. This article as a whole is about
    a. the moon.   c. distant planets.
    b. the sun.   d. the fact that the moon looks large from the Earth.

3. The word **it** in the second sentence refers to _____.

4. The air around our planet protects it.   Yes   No   Does not say

5. Which of these sentences are not true?
    a. The moon grows cold at night.   c. No new minerals were found on the moon.
    b. The moon is protected by air.   d. The moon seems large to us.
    e. Of all heavenly bodies, the moon is closest to the Earth.

6. What word in the fourth sentence means **people who travel in space?**

Getting Ready to Read

SAY AND KNOW

crops
lowlands
southern
level
wading
Research
    Institute
Philippines
develop
fertilize

Draw a line under each right answer or fill in the blank.

1. It means **low, flat ground.**　crops　bank　lowlands

2. **To be flat** is **to be**　southern　low　level.

3. **Walking in water** is　wading　leveling　cropping.

4. **The opposite of develop** is　fertilize　not grow　crop.

5. **Research** is　facts learned through study　a fertilizer　high land.

6. **An island nation in Asia** is the _____.

A-5　Food from Swamps

Rice is one of the most important food crops of the Far East. Much of it is grown in the warm lowlands of southern China.

The first step in planting rice is to make a level field. Next, a bank of earth about a foot (30 centimeters) high is built around the field. Then, water is poured into it. Workers put the small rice plants into the field by wading into the water in bare feet. As the rice grows, the fields must be kept wet and free of weeds.

In 1960, the Rice Research Institute opened in the Philippines. Here, researchers have developed new and stronger rice plants. They have found new ways to fertilize the

soil and make it richer. They have learned how to protect rice from harmful insects and diseases.

As a result, much more rice is grown now. In 1960, about 260,000,000 tons (236,000,000 metric tons) of rice were grown. In 1991, the crop was double that. There is still more work to do. The new rice does not grow well in some types of soil. Also, fertilizer is hard to get in some parts of the world. In the future, researchers will have to find ways to solve these problems too.

A-5 Testing Yourself

Draw a line under each right answer or fill in each blank.

1. Although not stated in the article, you can tell that
   a. if not enough rice is grown people may not have enough to eat.
   b. rice crops take a year to grow.
   c. rice is grown mostly in the United States.

2. This article as a whole is about
   a. farming in China.
   b. the Rice Research Institute.
   c. what we know about growing rice.
   d. floods in China.

3. The word **it** in the second sentence refers to _____.

4. Farmers plant rice seeds in the fields.   No   Yes   Does not say

5. Which two of these sentences are not true?
   a. Rice grows best in lowlands.
   b. Rice is a swamp crop.
   c. No new facts are being learned about rice.
   d. Rice is an important food crop in Asia.
   e. Rice ripens a few days after replanting.

6. What word in the first sentence means **food plants grown by people for their use**? _____

13

Getting Ready to Read

SAY AND KNOW

discovered
fuel
natural
amounts
surface
usually
petroleum
removed
tanks
pipelines
cheap
efficiently

Draw a line under each right answer or fill in the blank.

1. **Something taken away** has been   **reached   discovered   removed.**

2. **The top of something** is its   **length   surface   fuel.**

3. **The opposite of expensive** is   **best   natural   cheap.**

4. **Using efficiently** means
      making good use of   removing   using most of the time.

5. **A kind of oil** is   **pipeline   petroleum   tank.**

6. **A material that is burned for heat or power** is called _____.

A-6   Fuel Problems

In the last hundred years, we have discovered how to use natural gas for cooking and heating. The United States has large amounts of this fuel, most of it thousands of feet below Earth's surface. Natural gas is usually found where petroleum, the oil from which gasoline is made, is found. Often it must be removed before the oil can be reached.

Once we learned how to store natural gas in tanks and move it from place to place through long pipelines, we used it freely for lighting, cooking, and heating. At first, it was cheap. As we used more of it, however, prices went up.

Recently, we have learned new ways to find natural gas. We now have computers that can "see" under Earth's surface. These computers have helped us find more gas. With more gas available, prices have

14

gone down again.

Even so, we must use fuel more carefully. We must mine and use coal more efficiently. We must make better use of water and wind power. We can also find more efficient ways to use power from the sun to heat our homes.

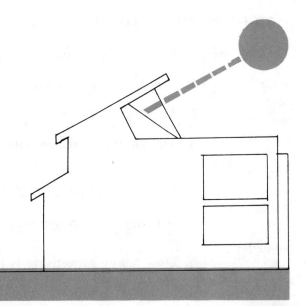

A-6　Testing Yourself

NUMBER RIGHT

Draw a line under each right answer or fill in each blank.

1. Although not stated in the article, you can tell that
  a. natural gas is useless.　　　b. wasting fuel is expensive.
　　　　　c. natural gas is moved in trucks.

2. This article as a whole is about
  a. discovering natural gas.　　　c. using natural gas.
  b. finding petroleum.　　　　　d. fuel and its uses.

3. The word **it** in the first paragraph, second sentence, refers to _____.

4. All states have natural gas.　　Yes　　No　　Does not say

5. Which two of these sentences are not true?
  a. Natural gas is not used.
  b. Computers are used in the search for natural gas.
  c. Natural gas is not used for heat.
  d. We must not depend on oil and gas for all our fuel needs.
  e. Natural gas can be stored.

6. What word in the fourth paragraph, second sentence, means **not wastefully**?

_____

Getting Ready to Read

SAY AND KNOW

weight
scale
ounce
kilogram
gram
depend
ton
liquid
liter
centimeter
meter

Draw a line under each right answer or fill in the blank.

1. It is **a unit of measure.**   ounce   weight   scale

2. **The opposite of solid** is   **depend**   **ton**   **liquid.**

3. **The amount paid on something sent by mail** is
                                          ton   weight   postage.

4. **Gram** is the last part of the word   **kilogram**   **meter**   **centimeter.**

5. It is **used for weighing.**   scale   liter   centimeter

6. **How heavy something is** is its _____.

A-7   Many Measures

We use different kinds of measures for different things. Many things you buy, for example, are measured by weight. Before you buy them, they are weighed on scales that measure weight in pounds and ounces, or kilograms and grams. A kilogram is 1000 grams, or a little more than 2 pounds. You would pay about twice as much for a kilogram of meat as for a pound of meat.

Both heavy and light things may be paid for by weight. The amount of postage you put on a letter depends on its weight. Coal, too, is paid for by weight. A ton of coal is 2000 pounds, or a bit less than 1000 kilograms.

Gasoline and milk, which are liquids, are measured in liquid measures. A gallon, a quart, and a liter, which is a little more than a quart, are all liquid measures. Smaller liquid measures are used for cottage cheese and sour cream. As a rule, these foods are sold by pints or half liters.

We use measures of length as well as measures of weight and liquid. We may buy ribbon by the inch or yard, or by the centimeter and meter. A centimeter is a little more than ⅓ of an inch. A meter is 100 centimeters. How many inches would that be?

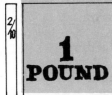

1 POUND

1 KILOGRAM

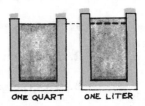

ONE QUART   ONE LITER

1 POUND

TWO and ²⁄₁₀ POUNDS EQUALS ONE KILOGRAM

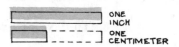

ONE INCH
ONE CENTIMETER

A-7 Testing Yourself

NUMBER RIGHT

Draw a line under each right answer or fill in each blank.

1. Although not stated in the article, you can tell that
    a. a kilogram is not a liquid measure.   b. milk is sold by grams.
        c. measure of length and liquid measure are the same.

2. This article as a whole is about
    a. selling coal.   c. several kinds of measures.
    b. weighing mail.   d. measures of length.

3. The word **them** in the first paragraph, third sentence, refers to

                                               _____.

4. All scales measure weight in kilograms as well as pounds.   Yes   No   Does not say

5. Which two of these sentences are not true?
    a. Most things use the same measures.   c. Milk is liquid.
    b. Many things are measured by weight.   d. Cost always depends on weight.
            e. The weight of a thing may determine its cost.

6. What word in the first paragraph means **a weight that equals a little more than**

  2 pounds? _____

Getting Ready to Read

striped
serve
bleeding
cure
represent
bandage
patient
beard
shave
trim
chief
specialize

Draw a line under each right answer or fill in the blank.

1. **To make well** is **to**   bandage   trim   cure.

2. It means **most important.**   chief   beard   striped

3. **To give service** means **to**   shave   represent   serve.

4. **To stand for** is **to**   represent   cure   trim.

5. **Losing blood** is   patient   striped   bleeding.

6. **To develop special skill in doing one thing** is **to**

_____.

A-8   The Bandage Pole

Do you know how the red and white striped pole became the sign of a barbershop? Many years ago, barbers not only cut hair but also served as doctors. Their main work as doctors was bleeding people. At

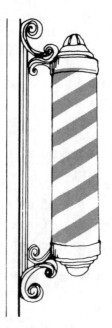
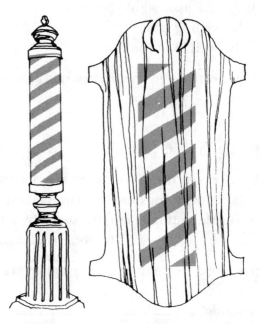

that time, it was believed that bleeding helped cure the sick. The white stripes on the pole represent the bandages with which barbers wrapped patients after bleeding them. The red stripes represent the blood. Long ago, a basin hung beneath the striped pole. This basin stood for the real basin used by barbers to catch the blood. Although barbers no longer do this kind of work, many have kept the bandage sign.

Our word *barber* comes from "barba," a very old word meaning "beard." Barbers still shave and trim men's beards. Their chief work, however, is cutting hair. When women first began having their long hair cut, they went to barber shops. After shops that specialized in cutting women's hair appeared, barbers served mostly men. Today another change is happening. Many barber shops now cut women's hair again.

A-8 Testing Yourself

NUMBER RIGHT

Draw a line under each right answer or fill in each blank.

1. Although not stated in the article, you can tell that
   a. bleeding is a good cure.   b. barbers serve mostly men.
           c. signs sometimes outlast their meanings.

2. This article as a whole is about
   a. barbers.   c. early doctors.
   b. getting a haircut.   d. barbers and their poles.

3. The word **their** in the second paragraph, third sentence, refers to

   _____.

4. "Barba" is an old word meaning "barber."   Yes   No   Does not say

5. Which two of these sentences are not true?
   a. Barbers no longer are doctors.   c. Women may use barbers.
   b. Barbers still trim beards.   d. Barber poles are all red.
           e. The sign of a doctor today is a striped pole.

6. What word in the fifth sentence means **cloth for covering a wound?**

   _____

Getting Ready to Read

industrial
engineer
factory
worker
obtain
education
adviser
president
escape
guide
dangerous

Draw a line under each right answer or fill in the blank.

1. An industrial engineer studies

   presidents   education   factory workers.

2. It means **to get** or **to gain.**   **obtain   escape   guide**

3. **Someone who helps to decide what should be done** is

   an adviser   an engineer   a guide.

4. **To show the way** is **to   obtain   escape   guide.**

5. **The opposite of dangerous** is   **education   industrial   safe.**

6. **The leader of our country** is the _____.

A-9   Using Time Wisely

Lillian and Charles Gilbreth were industrial engineers. They did not study engines. They studied factory workers to see how they could do jobs faster and better. They also taught their 12 children to use time wisely. In that large family, everyone helped to get the work done.

Many of our leaders learned early to use their time wisely. Mary McLeod Bethune, who was one of 17 children, studied hard in her

20

youth so that she could help others obtain an education. In 1904, she opened a school in Florida for black girls and boys. Later, she became an adviser to the President of the United States.

Harriet Tubman was born into a slave family in Maryland. But she escaped to the North in 1849. She went back South 19 times and guided 300 slaves to freedom. The trips were dangerous. But Harriet Tubman thought that helping others was making the best use of her time.

We use time to work, to learn, to help. Sometimes we use it to look at the sky and think or dream. Is that a good way to use time?

A-9 Testing Yourself

NUMBER RIGHT

Draw a line under each right answer or fill in each blank.

1. Although not stated in the article, you can tell that
    a. people have different ideas about using time wisely.
    b. all great leaders used time wisely in their youth.
    c. work is the only good way to use time.

2. This article as a whole is about
    a. Mary McLeod Bethune's girlhood.　　c. Lillian and Charles Gilbreth.
    b. schools for black children.　　d. making good use of time.

3. The word **who** in the second paragraph, second sentence, refers to

_____.

4. Many of our leaders did well in school.　　Yes　　No　　Does not say

5. Which two of these sentences are not true?
    a. Children of large families always learn to work hard.
    b. A child of slaves may lead others to freedom.
    c. A trained person can help workers do more in less time.
    d. The head of a school for black children can advise a president.
    e. Harriet Tubman never escaped from slavery.

6. What word in the first sentence means **having to do with factories?**

_____

An Adventure with an Alligator

One day in March, my friend Charles and I were traveling in a small boat up a body of water. We were looking for water turkeys and other interesting animals. Charles was in the bow of the boat. Suddenly, he called my attention to something moving in the water about 400 meters ahead. A large animal had put out from the bank. We knew that the animal was an alligator.

Wanting to get a good look at it, we went on slowly for some minutes. When we were about 300 meters from the point at which the animal had started, we headed for shore.

My friend stepped out onto the bank. I was about to follow him, but I happened to turn my head. There I saw the large alligator gliding straight toward us. It was moving as fast as a hungry alligator can, and that is fairly fast. A great black head and several meters of rough back showed above the water. The boat and I drifted a little way from the shore.

I remembered that I had no weapon. I knew that the animal could smash the little boat with a blow of its powerful tail. I knew it could crush me in its jaws.

I sat quite still in the boat, watching it come. It was not terribly large. But, the nearer it came, the bigger it looked. Those 3 meters of armor-plated body appeared to me not less than 6 meters.

The black head with its raised eyes and nostrils seemed huge.

Charles turned around and saw this alligator charging me. He did not know that I realized what was going on. He began to shout at me. I shook my head to quiet him. The alligator saw me move. It quickly sank beneath the water.

My adventure shows in an unusual way something of alligator life that is little known. You see, I was never in any danger. Alligators do not attack people unless threatened or cut off from some body of water that they are trying to reach. The alligator had no idea that it was charging a person. Lying far out in the water, it saw something against the bank. It noticed movement. It may have thought this thing near the shore was a wild hog. Hungry after a long winter fast, it had started to charge without taking time to be sure.

Adapted from Herbert R. Sass

MY READING TIME ⎯⎯⎯⎯ **(420 WORDS)**

Thinking It Over

1. Why did the alligator stop its attack?

2. Do you think the storyteller knew all along that the alligator would not attack him? Give reasons for your answer.

3. If the alligator had attacked, how might the storyteller have escaped?

Getting Ready to Read

SAY AND KNOW

branches
common
marsh
sack
pouch
throat
rely
safety
surroundings
blend

Draw a line under each right answer or fill in the blank.

1. **Usual** means   **sack**   **blend**   **common.**

2. **To depend on** is to   **rely on**   **branch out**   **blend in.**

3. **Soft, wet land** is called   **branches**   **marsh**   **pouch.**

4. **A bag** may be called **a**   **throat**   **marsh**   **pouch.**

5. **Widely found** means   **marsh**   **safety**   **commonly.**

6. **Things that are around something** are its _____.

B-1   Tree-Climbing Frogs

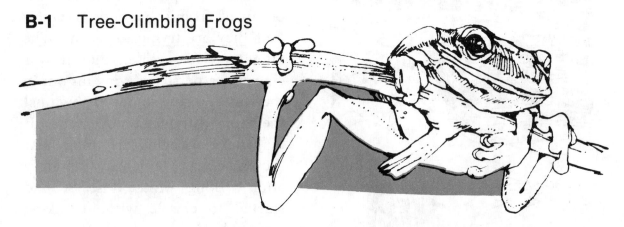

Have you ever seen a frog up in a tree? Several kinds of frogs do live in trees. They are able to climb and jump about because they have a sucker at the end of each toe. Using these, the frog can hold safely onto tree trunks and branches.

One of the most common tree frogs in the United States is called the peeper. Peepers are mostly found in swamps and marshes. They are usually not more than half a thumb length. The peeper has a sack, called a pouch, in its throat. In order to croak, it fills the pouch with as much air as it will hold. As the frog lets the air out, it makes a loud, croaking noise.

Tree frogs rely for safety on their skin coloring. They blend in with the colors of their surroundings. Many other animals are colored in ways that keep them safe. Can you name any of these animals?

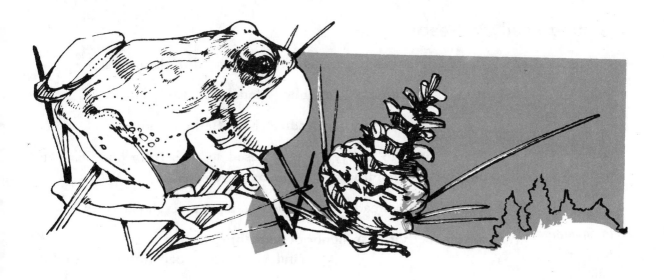

B-1 Testing Yourself

Draw a line under each right answer or fill in each blank.

1. Although not stated in the article, you can tell that
      a. peepers do not like water.   b. peepers live in water.
           c. peepers are not the only tree frogs.

2. This article as a whole is about
      a. large tree frogs.   c. safety for tree frogs.
      b. swamps and marshes.   d. peepers and other tree frogs.

3. The word **they** in the third sentence refers to _____.

4. Peepers usually live near swamps.   Yes   No   Does not say

5. Which two of these sentences are not true?
      a. Peepers croak softly.   c. Peepers are about half a thumb length.
      b. Peepers live in trees.   d. Peepers are rare in the United States.
           e. Tree frogs rely on their skin coloring for safety.

6. What word in the third paragraph, second sentence, means **mix in with?**

_____

Getting Ready to Read

SAY AND KNOW

India
celebration
Hindu
smear
battle
squirt
pajamas
independence
New Delhi
military
vehicles

Draw a line under each right answer or fill in the blank.

1. It means **freedom.**   republic   independence   battle

2. It is **a large country.**   Hindu   New Delhi   India

3. **Things used to carry,** or **things used to take from one place to another** are   military   pajamas   vehicles.

4. **To rub** or **to spread** is **to**   smear   squirt   vehicle.

5. **Special activities in honor of something** means
                                    independence   celebration   Hindu.

6. **To force liquid through an opening** is to _____.

B-2   Two Indian Celebrations

In India, one of the most joyful of all holidays is an old Hindu spring holiday called Holi. To celebrate the holiday, many people dress in white suits that look like our pajamas. People sing and dance in the streets. They throw colored water and colored powder at one another. Play battles take place. The weapons are buckets and squirt guns. Soon, faces and clothes are smeared with many different colors.

In addition to celebrating such old holidays, the people of India celebrate new holidays as well. One is Republic Day. On

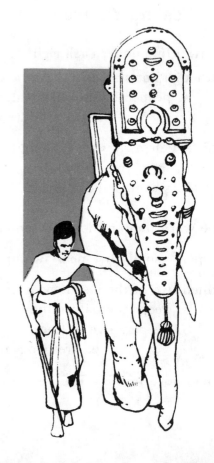

26

this day, a constitution was signed and a new government begun. A week-long celebration is planned each year at this time. On January 26th, a parade in India's capital, New Delhi, begins the celebration. Great crowds of people gather along a wide street called the Raj Path to see the parade. In this parade are elephants, bands, military vehicles, and marching school children. Dancers come from all over India dressed in clothes native to different parts of the country.

B-2 Testing Yourself

Draw a line under each right answer or fill in each blank.

1. Although not stated in the article, you can tell that
    a. Indians have few holidays.   b. India is a small place.
    c. in India, very old things exist along with very new things.

2. This article as a whole is about
    a. Republic Day.   c. two special holidays in India.
    b. Hindu celebrations.   d. pajamas worn in the streets.

3. The word **they** in the fourth sentence refers to _____.

4. India celebrates Republic Day in January.   Yes   No   Does not say

5. Which two of these sentences are not true?
    a. Holi is India's capital.   c. Holi is a Hindu holiday.
    b. India celebrates Republic Day.   d. Holi is in spring.
        e. People in India never celebrate.

6. What word in the second paragraph, sixth sentence, means **come together?**

Getting Ready to Read

moist
soil
earthworm
proper
condition
underground
loosen
search
decay
enrich
benefit

Draw a line under each right answer or fill in the blank.

1. It means **wet.**   earthworm   underground   moist

2. **To make richer** is to   condition   loosen   enrich.

3. **To make better** is to   search   loosen   benefit.

4. **Right** or **correct** means   soil   moist   proper.

5. **To look for** is to   search   loosen   benefit.

6. **To rot** means to _____.

B-3   Earthworms at Work

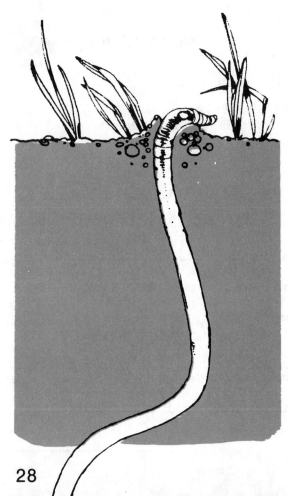

The best time to find earthworms is just after a rain. At that time, they come to the surface of the ground. If there has been no rain, earthworms can be found only in moist, loose soil.

Earthworms help to keep the soil in proper condition. As they crawl about underground, they loosen the soil. As they search for food, some of the earth enters their mouths and passes straight through their bodies. In this way, the soil is ground up and kept from getting hard. Air and water enter the ground through the tiny holes made by earthworms. The loose leaves and seeds that the earthworms pull into the ground decay. This enriches the soil.

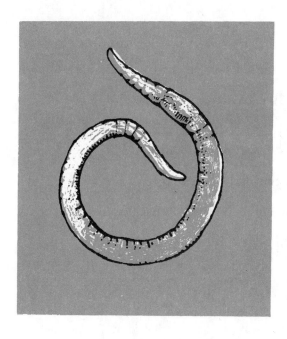

The work of one such worm, or even of a hundred worms, is not very important. However, many thousands of earthworms at work in an acre of land can greatly benefit the soil. Because of this, in places where there are not many earthworms, farmers sometimes buy them. They put them in the ground, hoping that they will live and enrich the soil.

B-3 Testing Yourself

NUMBER RIGHT

Draw a line under each right answer or fill in each blank.

1. Although not stated in the article, you can tell that
    a. earthworms are harmful.   b. farmers raise earthworms.
       c. earthworms are hard to find during dry weather.

2. This article as a whole is about
    a. finding earthworms.   c. earthworms and their importance.
    b. farmers and earthworms.   d. using earthworms for fishing.

3. The word **they** in the second sentence refers to _____.

4. Earth can pass through the body of an earthworm.   Yes   No   Does not say

5. Which two of these sentences are not true?
    a. Earthworms are important.   c. Earthworms live underground.
    b. Earthworms are not helpful.   d. Earthworms loosen soil.
      e. Earthworms are usually found on the ground's surface.

6. What word in the third paragraph, second sentence, names **a measure of land?**

_____

Getting Ready to Read

SAY AND KNOW

located
strangely
cryolite
climate
population
occupied
graphite
aluminum
Eskimo
cider
fertile
unsuitable

Draw a line under each right answer or fill in the blank.

1. **The people or animals who live in a place** are **its**

   climate   Eskimos   population.

2. **Lived in** means   **strangely   occupied   cider.**

3. **Found** means   **located   occupied   strangely.**

4. **It means unusually.   strangely   fertile   unsuitable**

5. **It is a light metal.   cryolite   graphite   aluminum**

6. **The kind of weather a place has** is **its** _____.

B-4   A Large Island

Located to the north and east of North America is a very large island that reaches almost to the North Pole. Strangely enough, this island, which is mostly covered by ice, is called Greenland. Some people believe that the place was given its unsuitable name by early settlers who lived on the coast and believed that the whole island was fertile and green.

Greenland was once settled by the Vikings. Later, the island came under the rule of Denmark. Because of the cold climate, Greenland's population has stayed small. Of its about 57,000 people, fewer than 15 percent are Danish. The rest are Greenlanders of Inuit origin.

Most Greenlanders live on or near the coast, where some grow crops. Others are occupied by sheep farming, graphite mining, and the mining of cryolite. Cryolite is used in making aluminum. In addition, Greenlanders gather the feathers, or down, of eider ducks. Eider down is used by many people in pillows and quilts.

Among the animals found in Greenland are polar bears, reindeer, foxes, and wolves.

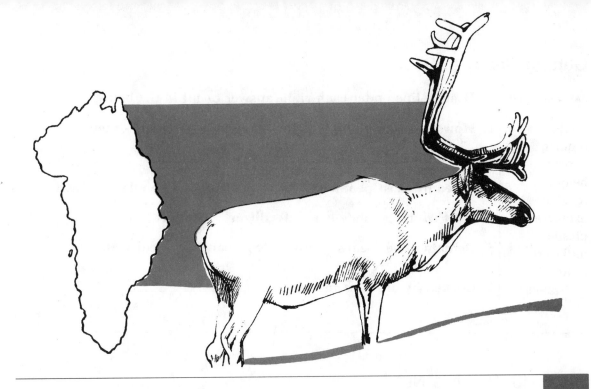

B-4   Testing Yourself

Draw a line under each right answer or fill in each blank.

1. Although not stated in the article, you can tell that
   a. life in Greenland has changed.   b. Denmark is cold.
   c. some Danish people were forced to live in Greenland.

2. This article as a whole is about
   a. Eskimos.   c. animals in Greenland.
   b. Viking settlements.   d. an island in the far north.

3. The word **some** in the third paragraph, first sentence, refers to

   _____.

4. Greenland was first settled by Danes.   Yes   No   Does not say

5. Which two of these sentences are not true?
   a. Greenland is a large island.   c. Crops grow near the coast.
   b. Greenland has large cities.   d. Greenland is warm.
      e. Most of the people in Greenland live near the coast.

6. What word in the first sentence means **land surrounded by water?**

   _____

31

Getting Ready to Read

popular
regular
survive
height
roasted
explosives
plastic
fertilizer
product
cultivated
cosmetics

Draw a line under each right answer or fill in the blank.

1. **How high something is** is **its**   height   product   regular.

2. **Usual** means   **regular**   explosive   roasted.

3. **Liked by most people** means   cultivated   **popular**   plastic.

4. **That which is made** is a   fertilizer   **product**   height.

5. **Remain alive** means   cosmetics   **survive**   cultivate.

6. **Cooked by dry heat** means _____.

B-5   Not Really a Nut

One of the most popular members of the pea family is the peanut, which in the United States is sometimes called the goober pea. Peanuts were first found in South America and have been cultivated for many centuries. Millions of kilograms of peanuts are grown each year throughout the United States. Large amounts are also grown in other parts of the world such as India, Africa, and China.

Peanuts grow best in loose, sandy soil. They require regular rain and cannot survive frost. After they grow to a certain height, the stems of the peanut plants bend over. The young pods are pushed into the soil.

The peanuts, or nutlike seeds, grow ripe under the ground.

Peanuts are used mostly for food. In the southern part of the United States, peanuts are used to feed farm animals. Peanuts may be roasted and eaten whole by people. Peanuts may also be made into peanut bread, candy, peanut butter, and other things. Parts of peanuts are also used in making oils, cosmetics, soap, explosives, plastics, fertilizer, and medicines.

The nut that is not a nut is a very useful product.

B-5 Testing Yourself

NUMBER RIGHT

Draw a line under each right answer or fill in each blank.

1. Although not stated in the article, you can tell that

    a. peanuts are costly.   b. peanuts are eaten in Japan.

      c. much work has been done to find uses for peanuts.

2. This article as a whole is about

    a. rare nuts.   c. the products made from peanuts.

    b. peanut oil.   d. peanuts and their uses.

3. The word **they** in the second paragraph, third sentence, refers to

                              _____ .

4. Peanuts are used mostly to make soap.   Yes   No   Does not say

5. Which two of these sentences are not true?

    a. Peanuts grow in dry lands.   c. Peanuts may be eaten.

    b. Peanuts grow underground.   d. Peanuts are really nuts.

      e. Peanuts have been grown for many years.

6. What word in paragraph four means **helpful?** _____

Getting Ready to Read

mighty
object
force
cliff
weaken
worn
ledge
support
gradually
action
seacoast
during

Draw a line under each right answer or fill in the blank.

1. **Little by little** means   **weaken   gradually   during.**

2. **The opposite of make strong** is   **weaken   ledge   worn.**

3. **Very strong** means   **support   mighty   seacoast.**

4. **Power** means   **mighty   ledge   force.**

5. **That which is done** is the   **object   cliff   action.**

6. **To hold up** means **to** _____.

B-6   Mighty Rock-Breakers

During a storm, mighty ocean waves often reach a height of over 30 or 40 feet (about 10 meters). These waves, made up of heavy weights of water, beat against an object on the shore. When they do this, something must give way.

In fact, even the force of smaller ocean waves changes the face of the Earth. Waves hit the base of rocky cliffs day after day. The rock begins to break. Over a long period of time, many small pieces of earth and rock are carried into the ocean. After many years, the lower rock may be weakened or worn away. Finally, the ledge above cannot stand without support. Then it, too falls.

Rock that is broken off in this way is often carried by the water to some other place. There it is deposited on the shore. The rock carried in this manner by ocean waves builds gradually. Over long periods of time, the breaking down and building up action of the waves causes many changes along the seacoasts of the world.

B-6 Testing Yourself   NUMBER RIGHT

Draw a line under each right answer or fill in each blank.

1. Although not stated in the article, you can tell that
      a. one wave can break a rock.   b. seacoasts never change.
          c. storms alone do not change a seacoast.

2. This article as a whole is about
      a. different seacoasts.   c. the cause of ocean waves.
      b. the strong ocean waves.   d. the action of ocean waves.

3. The word **they** in the third sentence refers to _____.

4. Rock broken by ocean waves becomes sand.   Yes   No   Does not say

5. Which two of these sentences are not true?
      a. The face of the Earth changes.   c. Waves are strong.
      b. Storms happen at sea.   d. The sea is always calm.
          e. Rock carried away by ocean waves is lost forever.

6. What word in the last sentence means **brings about?** _____

Getting Ready to Read

Draw a line under each right answer or fill in the blank.

1. **To grow** means **to**   develop   divide   imagine.

2. **Being born** is   conquest   numeral   **birth.**

3. **Not easy** means   develop   **difficult**   probably.

4. It means **one who lives in Rome.**   Roman   system   Arab

5. **Separate** or **break up** means   multiply   divide   difficult.

6. **Form a picture in your mind** means _____.

B-7   Two Numeral Systems

The numeral system we use today was probably developed by the Hindus many years before the birth of Christ. About A.D. 700, the Arabs adopted this system. It is called the Hindu-Arabic numeral system.

Some 2000 years ago, the powerful Romans used a different numeral system. Let us compare the two:

Roman:	I	II	III	IV	V	VI
H.-Arabic:	1	2	3	4	5	6

Roman:	VII	VIII	IX	X	L
H.-Arabic:	7	8	9	10	50

Roman:	C	D	CM	M
H.-Arabic:	100	500	900	1000

The Roman system is more difficult to use than the Hindu-Arabic system. As you can see, in order to write the Arabic 4 in the Roman way, we put I in front of V. In Roman numerals, 1984 would be written MCMLXXXIV. Can you imagine trying to multiply or divide using Roman numerals? Would it be easier to add or subtract using Roman numerals?

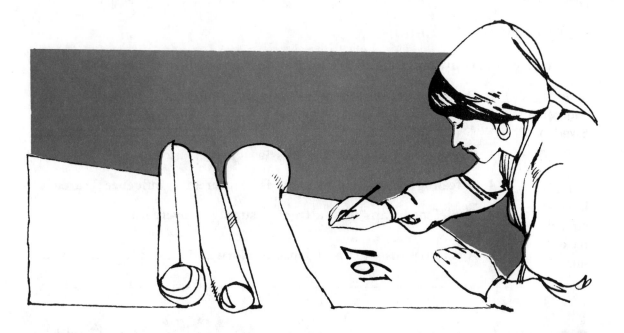

B-7 Testing Yourself

Draw a line under each right answer or fill in each blank.

1. Although not stated in the article, you can tell that

    a. Roman numerals are easy to use.   b. the Romans used zeros.

    c. people throughout history have needed ways to count.

2. This article as a whole is about

    a. Roman numerals.   c. why we use numbers.

    b. Hindu-Arabic numerals.   d. two kinds of numerals and how they differ.

3. The word **two** in the second paragraph, second sentence, refers to

_____ .

4. In the Hindu-Arabic numeral system, four is written IV.   Yes   No   Does not say

5. Which two of these sentences are not true?

    a. L means 60.   c. CM means 800.

    b. We use numerals.   d. It is hard to divide with Roman numerals.

    e. The Romans had their own numeral system.

6. What word in the first sentence means **in our time?** _____

Getting Ready to Read

area
overcome
Sweden
Norway
Russia
influence
interest
supply
nickel
attract

Draw a line under each right answer or fill in the blank.

1. **Power to act on others** is   supply   interest   influence.

2. **To draw to** is to   attract   supply   overcome.

3. **An amount of space** is   Russia   area   nickel.

4. **A feeling of wanting to know** is   interest   influence   area.

5. **To defeat** means to   attract   supply   overcome.

6. **A country just east and south of Norway** is_____.

B-8   The People of the Reindeer

Most of the people of Lapland have always lived spread out over a large area. They have lived as nomads. They travel about to find food for their large herds of reindeer. Because of this, it has been easy for some of their stronger neighbors to attack them.

In the ninth century, for example, the Lapps were overcome by the Vikings. In the sixteenth century, the Lapps came under the rule of Sweden. At other times, the Lapps were ruled by Denmark, Norway, or Russia. Of all these different rulers, Sweden and Russia had the most influence on the people of Lapland.

One reason that Lapland's neighbors have shown interest may be its rich supply of nickel and iron. Another reason may be the many ocean fish, such as cod, found in the northern seas off Lapland's coast. These good fishing grounds often attract fishing boats from Russia and Norway. Can you find Lapland on a map?

B-8 Testing Yourself

NUMBER RIGHT

Draw a line under each right answer or fill in each blank.

1. Although not stated in the article, you can tell that
   a. Lapps have lived close together. b. Lapps do not fish.
   c. Lapland is near Russia, Norway, and Sweden.

2. This article as a whole is about
   a. fishing near Lapland.   c. Lapland and its history.
   b. mining nickel and iron.   d. Lapland's neighbors.

3. The word **its** in the third paragraph, first sentence, refers to

   _____.

4. Norway overcame Lapland in the sixteenth century.   Yes   No   Does not say

5. Which two of these sentences are not true?
   a. England once ruled the Lapps.   c. Lapland has a seacoast.
   b. The Lapps are spread out.   d. Lapland is a southern country.
      e. The Lapps were influenced by the Russians and the Swedes.

6. What word in the first sentence means **a ground space?** _____

Getting Ready to Read

SAY AND KNOW

designed
materials
Italy
Italian
determined
solid
squares
cubes
triangles
rods
Montessori
cardboard

Draw a line under each right answer or fill in the blank.

1. **To design** is **to make in a certain way**   **to learn**   **to help**.

2. **A cube** is **a solid shape with six sides**   **a square**   **a triangle**.

3. **Determined** means **well known**   **helpful**   **not willing to give up**.

4. **Something hollow** is **not**   **empty**   **thin**   **solid**.

5. **Rods and cubes** are **materials**   **determined**   **Italian**.

6. **An Italian** is **from** _____.

B-9   A Determined Woman

In 1896, Maria Montessori was the first woman to become a doctor in Italy. But she became known all over the world for a different reason. She designed new materials to help children learn.

Maria believed that children learn best when they enjoy their work. In Italian schools at that time, small children had to sit still for hours. They learned letters and numbers by saying them aloud. Some children could not learn that way.

Maria was determined to find a better way. She started a school of her own and designed new materials for it. She made sets of cardboard letters that children could hold and move about. She made solid wooden squares, cubes, and triangles that fit into a board like puzzle pieces. She made rods of different lengths. The children could put these into rows from shortest to longest rods.

The children liked the new materials. They played with the cardboard letters and wooden shapes for hours. But they were not just playing. They were learning. Maria was able to prove what she believed. She showed that very young children can learn reading, writing, and arithmetic if they enjoy their work.

40

B-9 Testing Yourself

NUMBER RIGHT

Draw a line under each right answer or fill in each blank.

1. Although not stated in the article, you can tell that
   a. some children did learn by saying letters and numbers aloud.
   b. Maria Montessori started many schools.
   c. Maria Montessori did not like being a doctor.

2. This article as a whole is about
   a. Italian doctors
   b. well-known teachers
   c. how Dr. Montessori taught.
   d. schools in Italy

3. The word **them** in the second paragraph, third sentence, refers to

   _____   _____.

4. All children in Italy used the new materials.   Yes   No   Does not say

5. Which two of these sentences are not true?
   a. Children do not enjoy working.
   b. Maria Montessori started her own school.
   c. Small children cannot learn to read and write.
   d. Letters and puzzles are fun to play and work with.
   e. Maria Montessori proved what she believed.

6. What word in the third sentence means **things to be used?** _____

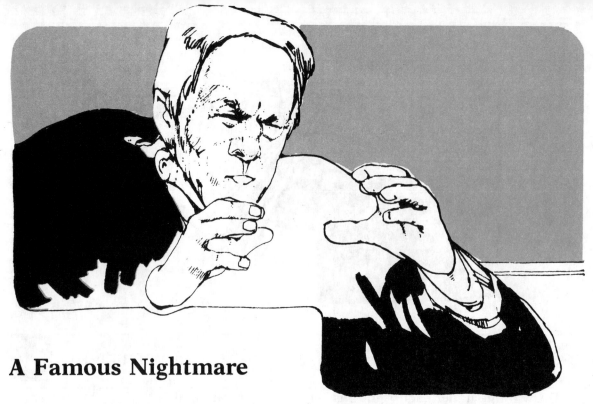

A Famous Nightmare

One night, more than 100 years ago, a young woman could not sleep. She was in her own room in a house beside a lake. Outside her window were the beautiful Swiss Alps. But her mind was filled with a different, frightening scene. This is how she described her dream, "I saw a pale student kneeling beside the thing he had put together. I saw the hideous phantasm of a man stretched out."

She went on: "The horrid thing stands at his bedside, opening his curtains, and looking on him with yellow, watery eyes."

The next morning the woman described the ghostly scene to the two people with whom she was sharing the lovely Swiss house.

One was her husband, the poet Percy Shelley. The other was the poet Lord Byron. Both men agreed that Mary Shelley's dream had the makings of a good ghost story. Lord Byron had already suggested that they write ghost stories to read to each other.

Mary Shelley took this idea seriously. Everyday she shut herself up in her room and wrote for hours. She wanted to write a book that would make her readers' spines tingle with fear. And she believed that her story could not fail to do that. It would be about a human being who makes a monster, a thing that has life. Mary Shelley believed that if people could do this, they would find the deed so terrible that they would run away from their monster. Then she asked herself, what would the thing do?

By now you may know the name of this ghost story. Mary Shelley named her book *Frankenstein*. Doctor Frankenstein was the person who was able to make a monster.

In Mary Shelley's book, Dr. Frankenstein does run away from his terrible monster. But the monster tells its maker that it would live in peace and never destroy anything anymore if only it had something to love. Dr. Frankenstein decides to make a second monster as a friend for the first one. But then he asks himself, what might two such living things do to people? Would making a second monster be too dangerous? Would it be too great a chance to take? He decides that it would be.

Mary Shelley's story was a success from the day it appeared. Since then it has been read by millions of people. It has been made into at least five motion pictures. Some of these movies are frightening. Others make fun of Dr. Frankenstein and his monster. But whether frightening or comic, Mary Shelley's nightmare lives on.

MY READING TIME _____ (420 WORDS)

Thinking It Over

1. Why was the young woman unable to sleep?

2. Why did Dr. Frankenstein not make a second living thing?

3. Do you think he was right? How do you think the monster felt?

43

Getting Ready to Read

SAY AND KNOW

Shetland
Scotland
shaggy
bushy
mane
originally
characteristic
breed
tough
gentle
gentleness
qualities

Draw a line under each right answer or fill in the blank.

1. It means **the opposite of rough.**   gentle   tough   shaggy

2. **At the beginning** means   bushy   originally   qualities.

3. **A kind** means a   mane   Shetland   breed.

4. **A quality of something** is a   characteristic   mane   shaggy.

5. **The hair on a horse's neck** is a   mane   breed   bushy.

6. **The quality of being gentle** is called _____.

C-1   Shetland Ponies

Shetland ponies are strong little animals that are less than 4 feet (about 1 1/4 meters) high. They have long hair, shaggy manes, and bushy tails. Originally, Shetland ponies came from the Shetland Islands, located north of Scotland.

The Shetland Islands have little grass or other plants. Fog, heavy winds, and long winters are characteristic of the area. In this difficult climate, the breed of small, tough ponies developed. They were so strong that the people of the islands used them in the mines to pull heavy carts filled with coal.

Shetland ponies, however, are not only tough. They are also gentle and patient. Because of their size and their good qualities, Shetland ponies were brought from the Shetland Islands to the United States. Some were used for children to ride. Some were sold to circuses and to fairs. Their pleasant looks, size, and gentleness soon made the ponies very popular.

Have you ridden on a Shetland pony or seen one at a circus?

C-1 Testing Yourself

NUMBER RIGHT

Draw a line under each right answer or fill in each blank.

1. Although not stated in the article, you can tell that
   a. Shetland ponies are from Scotland.   b. ponies are large.
       c. animals may grow differently in different places.

2. This article as a whole is about
   a. ponies from Scotland.   c. ponies in the circus.
   b. ponies as pets.   d. tough little ponies.

3. The word **one** in the last sentence refers to

   _____ _____.

4. Shetland ponies learn tricks easily.   Yes   No   Does not say

5. Which two of these sentences are not true?
       a. Shetland ponies are fierce.   c. The Shetland Islands are foggy.
       b. The Shetland ponies are small.   d. Children can ride Shetland ponies.
               e. The Shetland Islands have a warm climate.

6. What word in the second sentence means **rough?** _____

45

Getting Ready to Read

SAY AND KNOW

London
commerce
finance
nationality
occupation
historic
range
offer
subway
attraction
lovely
cathedral
parliament

Draw a line under each right answer or fill in the blank.

1. Your work is **your**   finance   occupation   nationality.

2. Something important from the past is
cathedral   range   historic.

3. Beautiful means   **range**   lovely   London.

4. A money matter means   lovely   **finance**   subway.

5. Business is   parliament   offer   commerce.

6. Something that draws us to it is an _____.

C-2   Let's Visit London

London, the capital of England, is another of the great cities in the world. It is also a very old city. It began nearly 2000 years ago in the days of the Roman Empire.

London is located on the River Thames and is near the Atlantic coast. It is one of the busiest centers of commerce and finance in the world.

People of many nationalities and occupations can be found in this historic city. In the shopping areas, there are fine things to buy. People travel about the large, busy city in subways or on double-decked buses.

At the center of London is Trafalgar Square with its tall statue of Admiral Horatio Nelson, a British hero. Other attractions for visitors to London include Buckingham Palace, the Tower of London, St. Paul's Cathedral, and the British Museum. There are many lovely parks and gardens. Many visitors go to Parliament to watch the British lawmakers at work in the House of Commons and the House of Lords.

C-2 Testing Yourself

NUMBER RIGHT

Draw a line under each right answer or fill in each blank.

1. Although not stated in the article, you can tell that
   a. London is located on the ocean.   b. London is a new city.
   c. sea trade probably helped London grow.

2. This article as a whole is about
   a. London, a large, busy city.   c. the capital of the U.S.
   b. commerce and finance.   d. Admiral Horatio Nelson.

3. The word **it** in the second sentence refers to _____.

4. Many Americans visit London each year.   Yes   No   Does not say

5. Which two of these sentences are not true?
   a. London is a large city.   c. London is 5000 years old.
   b. London is on the Thames River.   d. London is an Italian city.
   e. Buckingham Palace is located in London.

6. What word in the third paragraph, third sentence, means **underground railways?**

_____

47

Getting Ready to Read

insect
dragonfly
interesting
narrow
mosquito
destroying
perform
service
direction
hatch

Draw a line under each right answer or fill in the blank.

1. **Not wide** is   **direction**   **narrow**   **interesting.**

2. **Putting an end to** is   **destroying**   **performing**   **hatching.**

3. **Being useful to others** is called **being of**
                                   direction   **mosquito**   **service.**

4. One may walk in a   **direction**   **dragonfly**   **service.**

5. **To carry out** means to   **insect**   **hatch**   **perform.**

6. **Something that holds attention** is _____.

C-3   An Unusual Insect

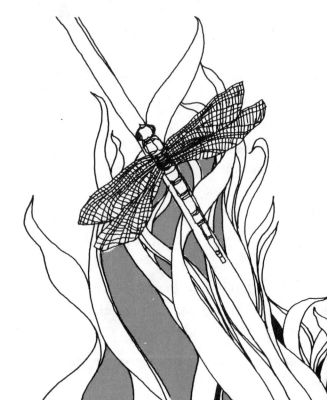

The dragonfly is a very interesting insect. Many people say that it looks like an airplane because of its large wings and its long, narrow body. It has two pairs of wings, one pair right behind the other. Dragonflies live around swamps and in places where the water is quite still. They eat mosquitoes and other small insects. They catch their food with their legs or jaws. In destroying mosquitoes, dragonflies perform a great service.

The dragonfly has big eyes made up of many smaller ones.

Because of this, dragonflies can see in almost all directions at the same time. When it sees an enemy coming, the insect can fly so quickly that it usually is able to escape.

The female dragonfly lays her eggs on the surface of the water or on plants just beneath the surface. As a rule, the eggs hatch within 2 weeks. Small dragonflies live under the surface of the water from 1 to 5 years. They change their skins many times before coming from the water as full-grown dragonflies.

C-3 Testing Yourself

NUMBER RIGHT

Draw a line under each right answer or fill in each blank.

1. Although not stated in the article, you can tell that
    a. dragonflies are dangerous.   b. dragonflies have short lives.
        c. dragonflies have unusual eyes.

2. This article as a whole is about
    a. mosquitoes.   c. an interesting insect.
    b. insects' compound eyes.   d. insects and swamps.

3. The word **ones** in the second paragraph, first sentence, refers to

                                  _____.

4. Dragonflies lay their eggs in water.   Yes   No   Does not say

5. Which two of these sentences are not true?
    a. Female dragonflies lay eggs.   c. Dragonflies have big eyes.
    b. Dragonflies live near water.   d. Dragonflies have two wings.
        e. Mosquitoes eat dragonflies.

6. What word in the last sentence means **adult?** _____

Getting Ready to Read

Missouri	Draw a line under each right answer or fill in the blank.

Missouri
Mississippi
stream
receive
builder
flood
shore
create
fertile
sediment
coarse

Draw a line under each right answer or fill in the blank.

1. **To get is to**   **receive**   **flood**   **stream.**

2. **One who builds is a**   **builder**   **shore**   **stream.**

3. **The opposite of fine is**   **flood**   **fertile**   **coarse.**

4. **It is land at the edge of water.**   **shore**   **flood**   **sediment**

5. **Rich soil is called**   **coarse**   **fertile**   **create.**

6. **Matter that settles to the bottom of the water is called**

_____.

C-4   Land Built by Water

The Mississippi River is a wide and mighty stream. It receives the waters of many other rivers and joins with the Missouri River to form one of the longest river systems in the world.

The Mississippi River is a great builder of land. During floods, it has left rich deposits of mud and sand along its lower shores. These deposits have created much fertile land for farming.

In addition, the Mississippi River deposits much sediment in the Gulf of Mexico. This sediment, carried to the Gulf year after year, has formed a delta, which is a land deposit at the mouth of a river.

This land deposit is shaped much like a triangle. It is named delta after the fourth letter of the Greek alphabet, which is also shaped like a triangle.

Mighty rivers depositing both coarse and fine materials at their mouths can build deltas as quickly as 1 foot (30 centimeters) per year. In the last 450 years, the amount of sediment deposited by the Mississippi in its delta has been over one half billion tons (or metric tons).

C-4 Testing Yourself

NUMBER RIGHT

Draw a line under each right answer or fill in each blank.

1. Although not stated in the article, you can tell that
    a. the Mississippi is long and narrow.   b. a delta is not fertile.
            c. rivers both break down and build up land.

2. This article as a whole is about
    a. large river systems.   c. a mighty river that builds land.
    b. the Missouri River.   d. the Gulf of Mexico.

3. The word **their** in the fourth paragraph, first sentence, refers to

_____.

4. The Mississippi River is part of a river system.   Yes   No   Does not say

5. Which two of these sentences are not true?
    a. The Mississippi is a land builder.   c. Land can build water.
    b. Rivers build fertile land.   d. Rivers create deltas.
            e. Deltas form at the sources of great rivers.

6. What word in the last sentence means **put down?** _____

51

Getting Ready to Read

SAY AND KNOW | Draw a line under each right answer or fill in the blank.

gathering

nectar

discover

hive

nourishing

delicious

replace

diet

1. **To put back** is to   **gather**   **replace**   **discover**.

2. Foods that keep us alive are   **nectar**   **nourishing**   **hive**.

3. Bees live in a   **hive**   **nectar**   **diet**.

4. **Pleasing to the taste** is   **diet**   **nourishing**   **delicious**.

5. **To find** is to   **diet**   **replace**   **discover**.

6. It means **the foods that people usually eat.** _____

C-5   Bees and Honey

Bees keep very busy all summer long. During this time, they fly from one flower to another, gathering nectar that they carry back to their hives. From the nectar, bees make honey. They store the honey in their hives. After the honey is made and stored away the bees use it as food.

Long ago, people discovered how good honey tastes. They began to take the honey that the bees were storing for their young.

Today many people raise and keep bees and sell the honey that they make. The people leave enough honey in the hive for the bees to live on during the winter. The rest is taken out and sold. Honey has enough food value to replace sugar in our diets. Because it is nourishing as well as delicious, a large amount of honey is sold every year in the United States. One year, for example, the amount of honey sold came to about ½ kilogram (over a pound) for every person in the United States.

C-5 Testing Yourself

NUMBER RIGHT

Draw a line under each right answer or fill in each blank.

1. Although not stated in the article, you can tell that
    a. bees get honey from flowers.   b. people cannot make honey.
         c. honey is sold in liquid form.

2. This article as a whole is about
    a. selling honey.   c. a nourishing food made by bees.
    b. bees and beekeeping.   d. raising bees for honey.

3. The word **they** in the third paragraph, first sentence, refers to _____.

4. Both old and young bees eat honey.   Yes   No   Does not say

5. Which two of these sentences are not true?
    a. Honey is nourishing.   c. People raise bees.
    b. Honey tastes bad.   d. Bees store honey in flowers.
         e. Bees make honey from nectar.

6. What word in the second sentence means **collecting**? _____

Getting Ready to Read

notice
colored
superstition
indicate
crystal
exist
belief
correct
partly
probable
bent

Draw a line under each right answer or fill in the blank.

1. **In part** means   **probable   partly   colored.**

2. **Expecting or fearing something without good reason** is
   crystal   superstition   notice.

3. **To show** means to   **exist   indicate   notice.**

4. **Not straight** means   **bent   correct   colored.**

5. **To be** means to   **belief   notice   exist.**

6. **Something likely to happen** is _____.

C-6   Ring Around the Moon

54

Have you ever noticed a colored ring around the moon? According to an old superstition, this ring always means that rain will follow. Another superstition says that the number of stars within the ring indicates the number of days in which it will rain.

Actually, the colored ring means that clouds containing moisture in the form of tiny ice crystals have formed several miles up. Rays of light from the moon pass through these ice crystals. This bends the rays. These bent light rays produce the colored ring.

However, such a ring can be seen only when the air has enough moisture. When other weather conditions also exist, these may combine with the moisture to cause rain. The belief, then, is partly correct. A ring around the moon means that rain is probable. The number of stars within the ring, however, has nothing to do with how long the rain will last.

C-6 Testing Yourself

NUMBER RIGHT

Draw a line under each right answer or fill in each blank.

1. Although not stated in the article, you can tell that
   a. superstitution may have some truth.   b. superstition is silly.
       c. a ring around the moon means that rain will follow.

2. This article as a whole is about
   a. superstitions.
   b. the moon and the snow.
   c. the meaning of the moon's ring.
   d. a sure way to know when it will rain.

3. The word **these** in the third paragraph, second sentence, refers to

   _____.

4. A ring appears only around a full moon.   Yes   No   Does not say

5. Which two of these sentences are not true?
   a. The moon's ring may mean rain.
   b. Light rays come from the moon.
   c. Rain comes from the moon.
   d. Bent light rays make rain.
       e. The moon's ring can be seen only when the air contains moisture.

6. What word in the first sentence means **given attention to?**

   _____

Getting Ready to Read

SAY AND KNOW

standard
standardize
vary
agree
accurate
length
accept
determine
fingertips
outstretched

Draw a line under each right answer or fill in the blank.

1. **Longness** means   **vary**   **length**   **standard.**

2. **The opposite of be the same** is   **agree**   **vary**   **accept.**

3. **Exactly right** means   **determine**   **standard**   **accurate.**

4. **Decide** may mean   **outstretched**   **standardize**   **determine.**

5. **According to rule** means   **length**   **agree**   **standard.**

6. It means **make the same all over.** _____

C-7 People Measures

Everywhere we look, we see people using measures. Most of these measures are standard. They do not vary from place to place. Everyone agrees that they are the same.

However, before our measuring systems were developed and made standard, people used less accurate kinds of measures. For example, measures of length were based on the parts of the body. Because the bodies of different persons varied in size, measures also varied. Even when people tried to standardize measures, different ones were accepted as right in different places.

In the early days, the length of a person's foot was used to measure distance in *feet*. The measure determined by wrapping something one time about the body was called a *girth*. A *fathom* was the distance between the fingertips of the outstretched arms. The distance from the tip of the thumb to the tip of the little finger of the spread hand was called a *span*. A *nail* was the length of the last two joints of the middle finger. A *palm* was the width of four fingers close together.

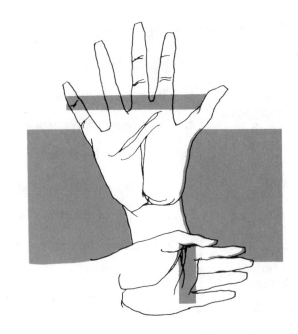

C-7 Testing Yourself

NUMBER RIGHT

Draw a line under each right answer or fill in each blank.

1. Although not stated in the article, you can tell that
    a. one modern measure is a *girth*.   b. early people needed measures.
        c. measures of length once were based on the parts of the body.

2. This article as a whole is about
    a. measures of time.   c. far distances.
    b. measures of length.   d. measuring parts of the body.

3. The word **they** in the third sentence refers to _____.

4. A *fathom* is the length of the foot.   Yes   No   Does not say

5. Which two of these sentences are not true?
    a. Most measures are now standard.   c. Few people use measures.
    b. Measures once varied.   d. Bodies vary in size.
        e. A *nail* is the distance between the fingertips.

6. What word in the first sentence means **sizes and amounts?**

Getting Ready to Read

steamboat
passenger
driven
engine
paddle
pilot
knowledge
dangerous
accident
explosion
interfere
extend

Draw a line under each right answer or fill in the blank.

1. **The opposite of safe** is   **knowledge**   **dangerous**   **driven.**

2. It is **a way of transportation.**   **steamboat**   **pilot**   **accident**

3. **Something used for rowing** is **a**   **pilot**   **passenger**   **paddle.**

4. It means **get in the way of.**   **dangerous**   **driven**   **interfere**

5. One kind of machine is an   **explosion**   **engine**   **extend.**

6. **Something that is not planned or wanted** is called **an**

_____.

C-8   Steamboating on the Mississippi

From about 1820 to 1870, many steamboats carried goods and passengers up and down the Mississippi River. These two-story boats were driven by wood-burning engines and large paddle wheels. The pilot was in charge of steering the boat on the ever-changing river. The pilot was the most important person aboard, even more important than the captain. It was upon

the pilot's knowledge of the dangerous river that the safety of everyone depended.

Most of the boats were so fancy that they were said to look like floating wedding cakes. Some had fine cabins, barbershops, dining rooms, and game rooms. Many of the boats, however, were poorly built. River accidents were common. Steamboats would often race from one point to another on the river. Each was trying to set a new record for speed. Sometimes, during a race, a boat's excited captain would take it to a speed that would cause an explosion.

During the Civil War, army travel on the river interfered with steamboat travel. After the war, railroads were extended, and land travel became much easier. Finally, the exciting days of steamboating on the Mississippi came to an end. Today, shipping continues on the river in large barges.

C-8   Testing Yourself

NUMBER RIGHT

Draw a line under each right answer or fill in each blank.

1. Although not stated in the article, you can tell that
   a. steamboats were popular in 1900.   b. land travel was once hard.
            c. steamboats were used mostly on the Ohio River.

2. This article as a whole is about
   a. trains and boats.   c. steamboat pilots.
   b. steamboat travel.   d. steamboat races.

3. The word **some** in the second paragraph, second sentence, refers to

_____.

4. Travel by steamboat was costly.   Yes   No   Does not say

5. Which two of these sentences are not true?
   a. Steamboats carried passengers only.   c. Steamboats used engines.
   b. Steamboats used paddle wheels.   d. Steamboats were fancy.
            e. Steamboats were steered by the captain.

6. What words in the last paragraph, third sentence, mean **stopped?**

_____

Getting Ready to Read

Draw a line under each right answer or fill in the blank.

1. **Things you remember** are **exciting** **famous** **memories.**

2. **Well known** means **importance** **famous** **successful.**

3. **A way of doing something** is called a **passage** **gift** **style.**

4. **Something given** is a **miner** **printer** **gift.**

5. **To take for your own** is to **adopt** **passage** **humor.**

6. Ability to find fun in things is _____.

C-9 A Famous Humorist

One of the best-known American writers is Samuel Clemens, whose pen name is Mark Twain. Born in 1835, Clemens grew up in the Mississippi River town of Hannibal, Missouri. As did many other young people of his day, Clemens dreamed of traveling on riverboats and of someday becoming a riverboat pilot. He used his memories of the life of a river town in his two most famous books, *Huckleberry Finn* and *Tom Sawyer.*

As a young man, Clemens held many jobs. He was a printer, a gold miner, and, for a time, he was a riverboat pilot. During his pilot days, he adopted the name Mark Twain. This was a term used on the

river to mean that the water measured 2 fathoms, or 4 meters (nearly 12 feet), which was deep enough for safe passage.

Finally, Twain became a successful writer. He traveled a great deal, writing and speaking. He became very popular both in the United States and in Europe.

Twain's style of writing was simple and direct. Among the things that he wrote about were superstitious people and people who were easily fooled. He used his unusual gift for humor to write about many things of importance.

C-9 Testing Yourself

NUMBER RIGHT

Draw a line under each right answer or fill in each blank.

1. Although not stated in the article, you can tell that
    a. Mark Twain means danger.   b. Twain wrote poems.
        c. Twain knew much about the Mississippi.

2. This article as a whole is about
    a. a riverboat pilot.   c. steamboat travel.
    b. a famous writer.   d. fooling people.

3. The word **he** in the second paragraph, second sentence, refers to

_____.

4. Two fathoms equal about twelve feet.   Yes   No   Does not say

5. Which two of these sentences are not true?
    a. Twain was successful.   c. Twain was a steamboat captain.
    b. Twain was a humorist.   d. Hannibal is a town in Mississippi.
        e. Mark Twain was a popular writer and speaker.

6. What word in the first sentence means **people who write?**

_____

A Nurse-General

Florence Nightingale was a famous English nurse who served in a great war. Because she carried a lamp as she visited wounded soldiers at night, she became known as "the Lady with the Lamp." But Florence Nightingale was much more than a nurse in the Crimean War. In many ways, she was more like a general.

When she and her staff of nurses arrived at the English Army hospital in Turkey, it was in a terrible state. As many men were dying of fever and disease as were dying of battle wounds. The hospital lacked supplies. It lacked medicine, bandages, and tools with which doctors could operate. It had no good kitchen ware. It had no good cooks to prepare food that sick people could eat. Worst of all, the hospital water supply was un-clean. The germs in it were spreading disease.

It may seem strange that the English generals let their soldiers grow sick and die without care. But the war was long and hard. Battles were fought in cold and rainy weather. Many soldiers had to go into battle before they were well trained. Supplies were often lacking. Battle plans were not always wise or wisely carried out. With so many problems on the field, it is not surprising that the generals did not know what was going on in the Army hospitals.

But Florence Nightingale was there, and she knew. And as matters got worse, she took charge. Money had been given to her in England for her work. With it she bought clean clothing for the soldiers and supplies for the hospital. She had the hospital scrubbed clean. She saw that clean bedding was used and good food served.

When the wounded overflowed the hospital wards, she had an unused wing rebuilt for their use. She saw that the hospital water was made safe to drink. After that, fewer soldiers died in the hospital. Almost none died of sickness caused by bad water.

The soldiers in that war were so grateful to Florence Nightingale that some of them gave her a puppy as a gift. The puppy took the place of another pet Florence Nightingale had loved. Before she became a nurse, she had tamed a baby owl and carried it around in her pocket. She could not carry the puppy in her pocket, but she took it back to England when the war was over.

Owls, as you may know, are supposed to be wise birds. We do not know if Florence Nightingale's pet owl was wise. There is no question, however, that it belonged to a very wise woman.

MY READING TIME _____ (420 WORDS)

Thinking It Over

1. Was Florence Nightingale a wise woman? Give reasons for your answer.

2. In what ways did she act as a general would act?

3. Do you think that "the Lady with the Lamp" is a good name for Florence Nightingale? Can you think of a better name?

Getting Ready to Read

SAY AND KNOW

immense
Pacific
depart
return
remaining
themselves
vulture
coyote
southern
Mexico
natural

Draw a line under each right answer or fill in the blank.

1. **The opposite of northern** is **Pacific**   **southern**   **Mexico.**

2. It is **a kind of bird.**   **coyote**   **Pacific**   **vulture**

3. **Staying** means   **remaining**   **themselves**   **return.**

4. **To go away** is to   **vulture**   **depart**   **return.**

5. It means **very large.**   **immense**   **depart**   **natural**

6. **To come back** means **to** _____.

D-1   Giant Turtles

Giant sea turtles must survive many dangers before they are full grown. These immense turtles are usually found in the Pacific Ocean. They lay their eggs about the middle of May each year. At that time, thousands of the big turtles may be seen on the warm, sandy beaches of southern Mexico. They are so close together that their shells often touch as they walk.

The eggs are deposited in a round hole that the turtles make in the sand. The mother turtle covers the eggs with sand. She pats it down with her feet and departs, never to return.

In addition to more natural dangers, the sea turtles have some

strange enemies to face. These enemies are people living near the coast who dig up the eggs, which are good to eat. They sell them for food.

In time, the remaining eggs hatch, and the tiny turtles set out for themselves. Many of them are then killed by vultures and coyotes before they even reach the water. Some of the turtles that finally do reach the ocean safely are later eaten by large fish.

D-1 Testing Yourself

NUMBER RIGHT

Draw a line under each right answer or fill in each blank.

1. Although not stated in the article, you can tell that
   - a. sea turtles are safe in water.
   - b. sea turtle eggs are big.
   - c. baby sea turtles must look out for themselves.

2. This article as a whole is about
   - a. animals of Mexico.
   - b. turtle eggs.
   - c. turtles and their eggs.
   - d. dangers for giant sea turtles.

3. The word **they** in the third paragraph, third sentence, refers to

   _____ .

4. Sea turtles lay eggs in the ocean.   Yes   No   Does not say

5. Which two of these sentences are not true?
   - a. Turtle eggs are good to eat.
   - b. Turtles eat coyotes.
   - c. Big fish eat small turtles.
   - d. Sea turtles lay eggs in February.
   - e. Sea turtles hatch on land.

6. What word in the last sentence means **without harm?** _____

Getting Ready to Read

SAY AND KNOW

abundance
herring
yield
Norwegian
visitor
harbor
mast
employ
prepare
fishing fleet
Lofoten
preserve

Draw a line under each right answer or fill in the blank.

1. **Great supply** means   **herring   abundance   yield.**

2. **To give work and pay to** is to   **preserve   ling   employ.**

3. **One who visits** is a   **visitor   Norwegian   fishing fleet.**

4. **To make ready** is to   **mast   prepare   employ.**

5. **To give** means to   **harbor   mast   yield.**

6. **A place of shelter, especially for ships,** is a

_____.

D-2   Fishing in Norway

Many people in Norway gain their living from the sea. Norway's long coast has an abundance of fish, among them cod, ling, and herring. The fish yield a large supply of food to the Norwegian people.

Early in the morning, a visitor to Norway would see the fishing boats leave for the day's work. In February and March, thousands of such boats from every part of the country make their way to the Lofoten Islands. There, for a short time, they stop at the harbor at

Bodo. The masts of the fishing boats at Bodo stretch as far as the eye can see.

The fishing fleet goes to Bodo to catch the cod. The fish arrive in great numbers on the coasts of the Lofoten Islands at that time of year. When the fish come near the shore, the boats sail out and the fish are caught in nets. After this, the fish must be cleaned and preserved and prepared for sale. Many people are employed in catching and preparing cod alone.

D-2 Testing Yourself

NUMBER RIGHT

Draw a line under each right answer or fill in each blank.

1. Although not stated in the article, you can tell that
    a. fishing boats have motors.   b. fishing is hard work.
           c. Bodo is in the Lofoten Islands.

2. This article as a whole is about
    a. a food in Norway.   c. supplying fish for Norway.
    b. catching cod.   d. Bodo harbor.

3. The word **they** in the second paragraph, third sentence, refers to

_____.

4. Fishing fleets go to Bodo to catch herring.   Yes   No   Does not say

5. Which two of these sentences are not true?
    a. Norway is on the sea.   c. Cod are not found in the north.
    b. Norwegians eat fish.   d. Fish are hard to find in Norway.
          e. Cod are caught in nets.

6. What word in the first sentence means **get?** _____

Getting Ready to Read

Draw a line under each right answer or fill in the blank.

tumblebug
manner
expect
finally
waste
material
barnyard
stable
beetle

1. It means **way of acting.**   material   waste   **manner**

2. **At last** means   **expect**   **tumblebug**   **finally.**

3. **An inside shelter for animals** is a   **barnyard**   **stable**   **tumblebug.**

4. **Matter** or **stuff** is   **material**   **manner**   **beetle.**

5. **Something useless** is called   **material**   **waste**   **tumblebug.**

6. **To look for** or **wait for** is to _____.

D-3   Tumblebugs

Have you ever seen two tumblebugs pushing a ball down a country road? This really happens. The tumblebugs are beetles, and they are not only playing a game with the ball. One of the beetles is in front of the ball and one is behind it. They push and pull in a manner that you would never expect. Sometimes, both of them fall over, but they keep at their jobs. Finally, they find a moist spot in the ground. Here they dig a hole with their feet. They put the ball into the hole, cover it up, and leave, never to return.

Why do you suppose tumblebugs do all this? The ball is composed of waste material left in the barnyard or on the stable floor by

68

animals. In this ball, the mother tumblebug has laid eggs. Warm and safe inside the ball, the baby tumblebugs live on the waste material until they are big enough to come to the top of the ground.

D-3 Testing Yourself

NUMBER RIGHT

Draw a line under each right answer or fill in each blank.

1. Although not stated in the article, you can tell that
      a. tumblebugs are beetles.   b. tumblebugs have many children.
          c. tumblebugs do not stay with their baby beetles.

2. This article as a whole is about
      a. tumblebug eggs.   c. tumblebugs caring for their eggs.
      b. baby beetles.   d. a road in the country.

3. The word **they** in the last sentence refers to

                _____ _____.

4. Baby tumblebugs live beneath ground.   Yes   No   Does not say

5. Which two of these sentences are not true?
      a. Tumblebugs stay with their eggs.   c. The baby bugs eat waste.
      b. Tumblebugs dig with their feet.   d. Tumblebugs are beetles.
          e. Tumblebugs carry the ball of waste on their backs.

6. What word in the first sentence means **pressing against?**

                                   _____

Getting Ready to Read

independent
Morocco
contrasts
desert
oases
oasis
permanent
flows
traveler
herder
high-tech

Draw a line under each right answer or fill in the blank.

1. **In a desert, places with water** are called   **oases   oasis   contrasts.**

2. **Lasting** means   **high-tech   independent   permanent.**

3. **A liquid that moves   flows   contrasts   herds.**

4. **A nation in northwestern Africa** is   **Desert   Spanish   Morocco.**

5. **A country that rules itself** is   **high-tech   permanent   independent.**

6. **A person who cares for a flock of animals is a** _____.

D-4   Land of Contrasts

The independent country of Morocco in North Africa is a land of contrasts. It has mountains and desert plains, ocean ports and inland cities. It also has oases, spots of green land in the desert where water is found. In these oases, grass, trees, grain, and fruit of many kinds can be grown. People can set up permanent homes in an oasis. They cannot do this in the empty desert around it.

The water in an oasis flows from underground springs. Sometimes, it is hot and must be cooled before it can be used. To the traveler, this fresh spring water is a welcome contrast to the hot, dry air of the desert.

Morocco also has contrasts of old and new. In the mountains, keepers of sheep, cattle, and goats may live in tents, as Moroccan herders have done for many hundreds of years. Many Moroccan city-dwellers live in sun-baked clay homes built hundreds of years ago. However, other Moroccans live in modern apartment buildings, some of them built when Morocco was ruled by the Spanish and French.

In recent years the cities have grown. Casablanca, Morocco's most modern city, is home to many high-tech businesses. Even here, however, you can see Morocco's rich history in the mixture of buildings that line its streets.

D-4 Testing Yourself

NUMBER RIGHT

Draw a line under each right answer or fill in each blank.

1. Although not stated in the article, you can tell that
   a. desert tribes lived in Morocco before the French and Spanish.
   b. fruit and grain can be grown in oases.
   c. sun-baked clay is used for some Moroccan homes.

2. This article as a whole is about
   a. people in an oasis.   c. Morocco.
   b. underground springs.   d. oases in Morocco.

3. The word **it** in the first paragraph, second sentence, refers to

4. Oases have good soil in which food can be grown.   Yes   No   Does not say

5. Which two of these sentences are not true?
   a. Part of Morocco is dry desert.   c. Oases have no water.
   b. Morocco is in North Africa.   d. People live in oases.
           e. Water from an oasis spring is always cold.

6. What word in the second paragraph, third sentence, means **different from what**

   it is being compared with? _____

71

Getting Ready to Read

Draw a line under each right answer or fill in the blank.

attain
diameter
contain
ripe
banana
cluster
valuable
consist
digest

1. **To hold inside** means **to**   **attain**   **consist**   **contain.**

2. **To reach** can mean **to**   **banana**   **diameter**   **attain.**

3. **To be made up of** means **to**   **consist of**   **cluster**   **digest.**

4. **The distance across the center of a circle** is the
   ripe   **valuable**   **diameter.**

5. **Things in a bunch** are **in a**   **diameter**   **consist**   **cluster.**

6. Once eaten, food is   **clustered**   **digested**   **attained.**

D-5   A Large Plant

The banana plant is one of the largest plants in the world. It sometimes attains a height of 30 feet (10 meters) and may be mort in diameter. Because of its unusual size, it is sometimes called a banana "tree." The stem of this plant, however, consists of leaves extending one over another. Because it contains no wood or bark, the banana plant is not really a tree.

Each banana plant produces only one bunch of bananas. The bunch is made up of a number of clusters, called hands. When the bananas reach the right size, these hands bay be cut off and packed for shipping.

As a food, bananas are very valuable. They may be eaten in place of potatoes or bread. If eaten before they are fully ripe, however, bananas are hard to digest. When ripe, the skin of the most common type of banana is yellow with small spots of brown. Care should be taken to choose only ripe bananas for eating.

D-5 Testing Yourself

Draw a line under each right answer or fill in each blank.

1. Although not stated in the article, you can tell that
   a. tree trunks always contain wood or bark.   b. trees are large.
          c. banana trees grow best in warm climates.

2. This article as a whole is about
   a. the bark of trees.   c. eating bananas.
   b. hands of bananas.   d. bananas and banana plants.

3. The word **they** in the last paragraph, second sentence, refers to

   _____.

4. Banana plants contain bark.   Yes   No   Does not say

5. Which two of these sentences are not true?
   a. Bananas grow on trees.   c. Bananas are best when ripe.
   b. Bananas grow in clusters.   d. Banana plants are small.
          e. Banana plants sometimes grow many meters high.

6. What word in the second paragraph, second sentence, means **a number of like**

   things growing together? _____

Getting Ready to Read

varying

simplest

separately

visible

sandstorm

roots

itself

algae

Draw a line under each right answer or fill in the blank.

1. **Something that can be seen** is   minute   visible   itself.

2. It means **most simple.**   roots   varying   simplest

3. **Very tiny** means   simplest   minute   sandstorm.

4. **One part of a plant** is   algae   visible   roots.

5. **Differing** means   itself   varying   visible.

6. **One by one** means _____ .

D-6   Colored Snow

Would you be surprised to see colored snow? Although snow itself is always white, it sometimes appears to be pink, brown, blue, or green! The most common cause of snow that seems colored is very small plants called algae, which have varying colors.

Algae are the simplest of all plants. Many of them have neither roots nor stems. Some of these simple plants live in the air. When snow falls, algae in the air may be carried down with it. The plants are too minute to be seen separately.

Only their color is visible. Because of this, it seems that the snow has changed color.

Another cause of colored snow is the red dust from sandstorms. This dust is sometimes carried hundreds of miles through the air. High in the air, it mixes with snow. When the snow falls, there is sometimes enough red dust mixed in with it to give it a pink color. In 1933, for example, a dust storm took place. Later in the year, dust from that storm caused snow falling in New England to look pink.

D-6 Testing Yourself

NUMBER RIGHT

Draw a line under each right answer or fill in each blank.

1. Although not stated in the article, you can tell that
    a. all algae live in air.   b. many plants have no roots.
        c. even very simple plants may have roots.

2. This article as a whole is about
    a. simple plants.   c. red dust.
    b. algae and sand.   d. things that color snow.

3. The word **which** in the first paragraph, last sentence, refers to

_____.

4. Snow itself is always white.   Yes   No   Does not say

5. Which two of these sentences are not true?
    a. Red dust makes snow blue.   c. Algae are animals.
    b. Algae are very small.   d. Algae may live in the air.
        e. Snow may look pink, brown, blue, or green.

6. What word in the last sentence means **made to happen?** _____

Getting Ready to Read

thermometer
speedometer
degrees
meter
temperature
Fahrenheit
Celsius
measuring
comfort
indoors
record
device

Draw a line under each right answer or fill in the blank.

1. **To write down** is to   comfort   record   degree.

2. **Amount of heat** is   meter   comfort   temperature.

3. **The opposite of discomfort** is   comfort   device   measure.

4. **A measuring device** is a   Celsius   meter   Fahrenheit.

5. **Finding the amount** means   recording   measuring   comforting.

6. Thermometers record heat in _____.

D-7   Two Scales for Heat

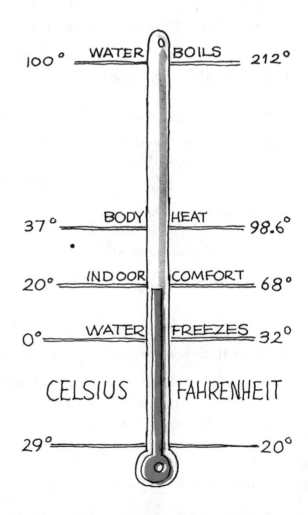

A meter is a measuring device. The meter in an automobile that records speed is called a speedometer. A meter that records heat or cold is called a thermometer. Thermometers tell us how warm or cold the air in a room is. They also tell us about body heat.

In America, we have long used a Fahrenheit thermometer. Most non-English-speaking countries use the Celsius thermometer. Both measure heat in degrees.

For comfort indoors, a room thermometer should read about 68°F, or 20°C. An oven thermometer measures oven heat from 200 to 550°F, or about 93 to 284°C. A body thermometer records normal body

76

heat at about 98.6°F, or 37°C. Still another kind of thermometer shows that water freezes at 32°F, or 0°C. An outdoor thermometer may record temperatures from 20 below 0 to 120°F, or from about −29 to 49°C.

A thermometer is a much-used measuring device. It proves helpful indoors and out. It is used in the home, the office, the factory, in parks, on boats, and in many other places.

D-7 Testing Yourself   **NUMBER RIGHT**

Draw a line under each right answer or fill in each blank.

1. Although not stated in the article, you can tell that
     a. thermometers are always right.   b. thermometers are hard to make.
           c. body temperature above 99°F is above normal.

2. This article as a whole is about
     a. speedometers.   c. outdoor thermometers.
     b. thermometers and their uses.   d. measuring heat and weight.

3. The word **they** in the fifth sentence refers to _____.

4. Water freezes at 35°F.   Yes   No   Does not say

5. Which two of these sentences are not true?
     a. Thermometers measure heat.   c. Heat can be measured.
     b. Thermometers are used outside.   d. Speedometers measure heat.
           e. Thermometers are used only indoors.

6. What word in the last paragraph means **often made use of**?

Getting Ready to Read

SAY AND KNOW

zinc
government
secretary
arranged
treaty
purchase
approve
jokingly
folly
proved
wonderful
acres
century

Draw a line under each right answer or fill in the blank.

1. **Foolishness** means   **approval**   **folly**   **treaty.**

2. **To buy** means **to**   **approve**   **prove**   **purchase.**

3. **A widely used metal is**   **acre**   **zinc**   **folly.**

4. **One kind of agreement is a**   **folly**   **secretary**   **treaty.**

5. **Set up** means   **proved**   **purchased**   **arranged.**

6. **A nation's system of rule is its** _____

D-8   A Good Buy

Alaska, which became the forty-ninth state of the United States in 1959, was bought from Russia in 1867. The price paid to the Russian government for this huge piece of land was $7,200,000. Secretary of State Seward arranged the treaty and the purchase. Because people in the United States at that time knew little about Alaska, many of them did not approve of purchasing it. Some jokingly called Alaska "Seward's Folly."

However, Alaska turned out to be a bargain. Gold was found there in 1896. Even after a century of mining, Alaska is still the main source of gold in the United States. Alaska also has the largest zinc and silver mines in the country. In 1968, oil was discovered in the state. The oil deposits are among the richest in the world. Alaska's streams and rivers are full of fish. Salmon caught in the state is eaten across the nation. Alaskan hills have thousands of acres of valuable timber. The state is also home to such animals as seals, sea otters, minks, foxes, and beavers.

If Seward were alive today, he would be proud of his purchase.

D-8 Testing Yourself

NUMBER RIGHT

Draw a line under each right answer or fill in each blank.

1. Although not stated in the article, you can tell that
    a. people know little about Alaska.   b. Alaska was always a state.
              c. Alaska still has unused wealth.

2. This article as a whole is about
    a. $7,200,000.   c. the United States and Russia.
    b. Alaska.   d. a secretary of state.

3. The word **it** in the first paragraph, fourth sentence, refers to _____ .
4. Alaska was a foolish purchase.   Yes   No   Does not say

5. Which two of these sentences are not true?
    a. Alaska has valuable timber.   c. Seward worked in government.
    b. Alaska was a good buy.   d. Alaska cost 2 million dollars.
              e. Alaska became a state in 1867.

6. What word in the last sentence means **living?** _____

Getting Ready to Read

SAY AND KNOW

siege
ancient
business
archeology
science
remains
prehistoric
methods
archeologist
history
Greek

Draw a line under each right answer or fill in the blank.

1. It means an **attempt to overcome.**   science   siege   method

2. **Very old** means   business   history   ancient.

3. **A body of known facts** can be called
an archeologist   a business   a science.

4. **Before we kept records** is called   ancient   Greek   prehistoric.

5. **Things that are left** are called   business   remains   science.

6. **A person's work** or **occupation** is **his or her** _____.

D-9   Digging for History

Homer's poem, *The Iliad*, tells the story of the 10-year siege of Troy by the ancient Greeks. If you have heard the story, you may remember that the Greeks left a huge, hollow horse outside the gates of Troy. Cassandra, the Trojan king's daughter, warned against the horse. But the Trojans did not listen. They took the horse inside the gates. That night, soldiers hidden in it destroyed the city.

In later times, people did not agree on where Troy had been. In 1868, a German named Heinrich Schliemann decided to find out. He had made a lot of money in business during the Crimean War.

He used the money to learn all that he could about Troy and other ancient cities. He also used the money to study archeology. That is the science of digging up the remains of early settlements.

In 1871, Heinrich and his wife Sophia, who was a Greek, began

digging for Troy. Heinrich and Sophia together directed the work of almost 200 diggers. But they dug up with their own hands beautiful metal tools and weapons from pre-historic times.

Later, archeologists improved on the Schliemanns' work and methods. But the metal tools, city walls, and other remains that the Schliemanns found were important to our study of Troy and of human history.

D-9 Testing Yourself

NUMBER RIGHT

Draw a line under each right answer or fill in each blank.

1. Although not stated in the article, you can tell that
   a. Homer was blind.   b. Cassandra was a Greek.
   c. we have much to learn about very old cities.

2. This article as a whole is about
   a. a famous poem.   c. the siege of Troy.
   b. digging for Troy.   d. Homer's famous *Iliad*.

3. The word **it** in the first paragraph, sixth sentence, refers to _____.

4. Heinrich Schliemann was German.   Yes   No   Does not say

5. Which two of these sentences are not true?
   a. The Schliemanns searched for Greece.
   b. The Schliemanns' work was important in the search for Troy.
   c. The Schliemanns worked together.
   d. The Trojans did not listen to Cassandra's warning.
   e. The hollow horse was a help to Troy.

6. What word in the last paragraph, first sentence, means **people who dig for the**

   remains of ancient settlements? _____.

81

Outwitting Brindle

Uncle Hyatt Frame bought a cow named Brindle. He was pleased with his new cow until he milked her for the first time. It took only 2 minutes for him to discover that she was a "switcher." Now, it is bad enough to have a cow that keeps her tail going in fly time. But in winter, there is no excuse for it. A blow in the face from a long, stringy tail is sure to cause a strong feeling leading to anger.

At the first switch of Brindle's tail, Uncle Hyatt shouted, "Hey!" At the second, he hit the cow in anger. At the third, he got off the milking stool, found a piece of rope, and tied the tail to a rafter.

Warm weather came. Uncle Hyatt moved his milking outside. At the first switch, he grabbed the tail and tied it to his boot strap. When he finished the milking, he got up and picked up the pail of milk. Then he gave Brindle a slap. Brindle moved away, taking Uncle Hyatt's left leg with her. His right leg followed.

Looking up from her work, Aunt Emily was amazed. She saw Uncle Hyatt hopping quickly about after the cow. Milk splashed from the pail. Aunt Emily had no idea what the trouble was. The only thing that she could see was that a whole milking was rapidly going to waste. She called loudly, "Look out for the milk!" Then she hurried to help.

By this time, Uncle Hyatt and Brindle had passed the farther end of the yard. They had even started on the return trip. Brindle had the air of someone who knew where she was going. Uncle Hyatt hopped after her, still holding the milk pail, which grew lighter and lighter.

"Stop her!" cried Uncle Hyatt.

Brindle was between them, so Aunt Emily did not know the reason for Uncle Hyatt's strange behavior. She ran through the gate, waving her arms and calling, "Whoa, Brindle!"

The frightened cow began to run. The milk pail flew off to one side. Uncle Hyatt fell and moved quickly along at Brindle's heels, grabbing at anything in sight.

Finally, his boot strap broke. Brindle ran to the farthest corner of the yard. Aunt Emily helped Uncle Hyatt to his feet, took him into the kitchen, and worked over him with liniment. "Tell me something, Hyatt," she said. "If you had to tie the tail to a leg, why didn't you tie it to Brindle's?"

Adapted from "Youth's Companion"

MY READING TIME _____ (420 WORDS)

Thinking It Over

1. Do you think Brindle knew what she was doing? What are your reasons?

2. Why did the milk pail grow lighter and lighter?

3. Do you think Aunt Emily's suggestion was a good one? Can you think of something else Hyatt might have done to avoid so much trouble?

Getting Ready to Read

SAY AND KNOW

worst
pest
flea
disease
plague
feared
roving
habit
enemy
thrive
rid
community
communities

Draw a line under each right answer or fill in the blank.

1. **Wandering** means   **roving**   **pest**   **disease.**

2. It means **the opposite of friend.**   **flea**   **enemy**   **pest**

3. **If people are afraid of it,** it is   **roving**   **scaly**   **feared.**

4. **To do very well** is to   **rid**   **thrive**   **plague.**

5. It is **a usual act.**   **scaly**   **worst**   **habit**

6. **People living together** form a _____.

E-1   Here Comes Trouble

In every part of the world, people consider the rat one of the worst animal pests. This has been true all through history. Rats not only do much damage to property, but they also carry fleas, and these spread harmful diseases. The bubonic plague, one of the most feared diseases, was spread over large parts of the world in this way.

Black rats and brown rats are the two main types of these animal pests. Both black and brown rats

have roving habits. By traveling in ships, they have spread from Asia and Europe to other parts of the world. Brown rats are the larger of the two. They are enemies of black rats and have driven them away from many areas. It is only when black rats travel to places that have no brown rats that they are able to thrive.

Because rats create real dangers to our health, we should do everything that we can to rid our communities of them.

E-1 Testing Yourself

NUMBER RIGHT

Draw a line under each right answer or fill in each blank.

1. Although not stated in the article, you can tell that
   a. a rat may harm another rat.   b. rats are bigger than cats.
          c. rats cannot swim.

2. This article as a whole is about
   a. brown and black rats.   c. rats in Asia.
   b. rats on ships.   d. the bubonic plague.

3. The word **these** in the third sentence refers to _____.

4. Black rats are larger than brown rats.   Yes   No   Does not say

5. Which two of these sentences are not true?
   a. Rats travel on ships.   c. Rats carry fleas.
   b. Fleas carry rats.   d. Fleas are helpful to people.
          e. The rat is an animal pest.

6. What word in the last sentence means **make** or **bring into being?**

_____

Getting Ready to Read

hook
metal
cord
prevent
gather
trained
household
obsolete
catch
cormorant
loose
remove

Draw a line under each right answer or fill in the blank.

1. It is a part of a bird.   cord   bill   metal

2. Keep from happening means   **prevent   train   gather.**

3. A bird taught to do something is   **prevented   trained   hooked.**

4. Something no longer done is   **obsolete   gathered   loose.**

5. Certain hard materials are   **cormorants   metals   households.**

6. The opposite of to leave in is to _____.

E-2   A Working Bird

A cormorant is a large bird with webbed feet, a neck, and a long, powerful bill with a hook at the end. The largest cormorants may be nearly a meter (more than 30 inches) long. Cormorants live on or near the water. They can stay under water for a long time when they dive for fish.

Cormorants can be trained to catch fish for people to eat. Fish-catching cormorants have long cords tied to their bodies and loose metal rings around their necks. Their keepers put the birds into the water, holding onto the strings. Then the birds begin to dive for fish.

When a cormorant catches a fish, it tries to swallow it, but the

86

metal ring on its neck prevents it from doing so. To gather the catch, the keepers bring the bird in by the cords. Opening the birds' bills, they remove the fish.

Fishing with trained cormorants used to be done all over Europe. In fact, the keeper of cormorants in England was an officer of the Royal Household. Today, this kind of fishing is obsolete in Europe. But it is still done in places near China.

E-2   Testing Yourself

Draw a line under each right answer or fill in each blank.

1. Although not stated in the article, you can tell that
   a. cormorants eat fish.   b. cormorants are used in the U.S.A.
              c. cormorants like only certain kinds of fish.

2. This article as a whole is about
   a. learning to fish.   c. water and shore birds.
   b. fishing in Europe.   d. using cormorants for fishing.

3. The word **they** in the first paragraph, fourth sentence, refers to

   _____.

4. The metal ring helps the cormorant swallow.   Yes   No   Does not say

5. Which two of these sentences are not true?
   a. Cormorants do not eat fish.   d. Cormorants catch fish.
   b. Cormorant fishing is still done   e. Cormorants are large birds
      in Europe.   with webbed feet.
   c. Fish can be eaten.

6. What word in the last paragraph, third sentence, means **no longer done**?

   _____

Getting Ready to Read

cockroach
baseboard
damp
crevice
whatever
female
fabric
airing
reduce
damage
creature
household

Draw a line under each right answer or fill in the blank.

1. **Slightly wet** means   **damp**   **airing**   **damage**.

2. **A crack** is called a   **fabric**   **crevice**   **baseboard**.

3. It is **the opposite of male**.   **female**   **creature**   **reduce**

4. **Woven material** is called   **household**   **whatever**   **fabric**.

5. It is **an insect pest**.   **creature**   **crevice**   **cockroach**

6. **Leaving something in contact with the air** is called

_____ .

E-3   House Pests

The cockroach is a common house pest. This insect lives in cracks, under floors, behind baseboards, or in dark, damp crevices. The cockroach does not like bright light. Because of this, cockroaches usually come out only at night. Then they eat whatever food or garbage they can find. Homes can usually be kept free of cockroaches by keeping the rooms clean and dry.

The clothes moth is another household pest. The female clothes moth lays her eggs in anything made of wool or of hair. These eggs hatch into caterpillars that eat the fabric around them. Moths, like

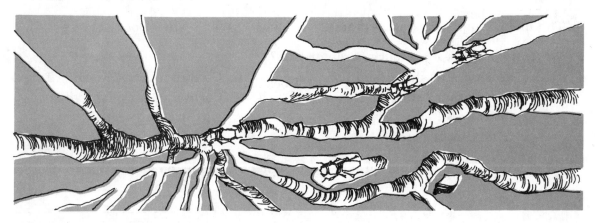

roaches, do not like sunlight or fresh air. So airing clothing and carpets in spring will help to reduce the damage done by moths.

Termites are pests that eat wood. These creatures often get into the wooden parts of a house. Here, they do a great deal of damage. To avoid termites, the wooden parts of houses should be built well above the ground. The parts of houses that do touch the ground should be made of stone, brick, or concrete.

E-3   Testing Yourself

NUMBER RIGHT

Draw a line under each right answer or fill in each blank.

1. Although not stated in the article, you can tell that
     a. some caterpillars become moths.   b. fresh air kills house pests.
        c. termites always stay underground.

2. This article as a whole is about
     a. three pests.   c. pests that eat wood.
     b. moths and termites.   d. keeping rooms dry.

3. The word **them** in the second paragraph, third sentence, refers to

_____ .

4. Caterpillars eat fabric.   Yes   No   Does not say

5. Which two of these sentences are not true?
     a. Moths love sunlight.   c. Cockroaches are pests.
     b. Termites eat clothes.   d. Clothes moths eat fabric.
        e. Cockroaches may feed on garbage.

6. What word in the first sentence means **not unusual**? _____

Getting Ready to Read

SAY AND KNOW

driest
border
range
vacation
tourist
canyon
remind
monument
unique
scenery
mineral

Draw a line under each right answer or fill in the blank.

1. It means **most dry.**   unique   driest   mineral

2. **Someone traveling for fun is a**   tourist   canyon   range.

3. **It is a row** or **a line.**   border   range   vacation

4. **Something that is one of a kind is**   remind   canyon   unique.

5. **Free time** means   monument   vacation   scenery.

6. **To help one remember** is to _____.

E-4 An Unusual Park

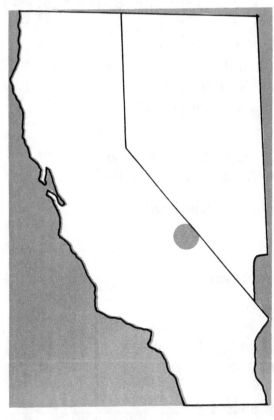

Death Valley, which is located in California, is the lowest, direst, and hottest place in North America. This famous spot is at the center of a very large park called Death Valley National Monument. The park itself is bordered by mountain ranges. It is noted for its beautiful, unique scenery. Because of this, Death Valley National Monument has become a popular vacation spot.

Many tourists each year come to visit this famous place. They come to see the valleys, canyons, desert sands, and high mountains. These different areas are all very close. Visitors can stand near Death Valley, parts of which are below sea level. In the distance, less than 100 miles (160 kilometers) away from Death Valley, visitors can see Telescope Peak, which is over 11,000 feet (3351.32 meters) high, and Mount Whitney, which is over 14,000 feet (4265.32 meters) high.

Tourists may be reminded of American history. A mineral called borax was mined in Death Valley in the 1880s. At that time, wagons pulled by 20 mule teams were used to haul the borax out of the valley.

E-4 Testing Yourself

NUMBER RIGHT

Draw a line under each right answer or fill in each blank.

1. Although not stated in the article, you can tell that
      a. Death Valley is large.   b. many tourists visit Mount Whitney.
         c. mule teams are no longer used in Death Valley.

2. This article as a whole is about
      a. borax mining.   c. an interesting place to visit.
      b. California.   d. tourists.

3. The word **they** in the second paragraph, second sentence, refers to

                                        _____.

4. Death Valley is in Colorado.   Yes   No   Does not say

5. Which two of these sentences are not true?
      a. Borax is a mineral.   d. Telescope Peak is higher than Mount
      b. Death Valley is hot.   Whitney.
      c. No land exists below sea   e. Death Valley National Monument is a
         level.   park.

6. What word in the last sentence means **pull?** _____

Getting Ready to Read

protein

cholesterol

calories

exists

recognized

value

recently

appreciate

enhance

expensive

Draw a line under each right answer or fill in the blank.

1. Something that happened **lately** happened _____.

2. A word that means **costs a lot of money** is

                                        protein   recognized   expensive.

3. To **add to** means to   **enhance   value   appreciate.**

4. **Fattening** foods have a lot of   **calories   protein   value.**

5. Two **food parts that can be bad for you** are fat and

                                        _____.

6. **Worth** means   **expensive   value   recently.**

E-5   The Wonder Bean

What if one small bean could be turned into "milk," "flour," "hamburgers," and even "ice cream"? What if it were rich in protein and easy to grow? What if it were low in fat and cholesterol and had fewer calories than meat? Wouldn't it be the wonder bean? In fact, such a bean exists—the soybean. People in Asia have recognized the value of the soybean for thousands of years. In the West, we have only recently began to appreciate the wonder bean.

Think of how soybeans might enhance just one meal. Soy meal might be added to your hamburger to

make it higher in protein, lower in fat, and less expensive. Soy flour could be used in the hamburger roll—again making it richer in protein. Soybean sprouts are a tasty (and crunchy) addition to your salad. The salad can be topped with a dressing or mayonnaise made from tofu—a cheese-like soy product. Tofu can also be used to create a dessert that looks, feels, and tastes very much like ice cream—but without the fat.

Enjoy your lunch!

E-5 Testing Yourself

Draw a line under each right answer or fill in each blank.

1. Although not stated in the article, you can tell that
   a. hamburgers are good for you.   b. you shouldn't eat too much fat.
               c. soybeans only grow in Asia.

2. This article as a whole is about
   a. wholesome diets.   c. the value of soybeans.
   b. how soy flour is used.   d. becoming healthier.

3. The word **it** in the second sentence refers to _____.

4. Soybeans contain protein.   Yes   No   Does not say

5. Which two of the following questions are not true?
   a. People do not eat soy products.   c. Tofu is made from milk.
   b. Ice cream is high in fat.   d. Soy flour costs less than meat.
               e. Bean sprouts are low in fat.

6. What word in the fifth sentence of paragraph one means **is**? _____

Getting Ready to Read

SAY AND KNOW

vessel
painful
shin
nerve
injury
observe
brittle
properly
heal
completely
fact

Draw a line under each right answer or fill in the blank.

1. **To make well** or **to grow well** means **to**   heal   observe   brittle.

2. **A container** is **a**   shin   vessel   fact.

3. **Doing something the right way** means **doing it**   properly   painfully   injury.

4. **Easily broken** means   completely   nerve   brittle.

5. **To notice** means **to**   heal   observe   nerve.

6. **Something that hurts** is _____.

E-6   Facts About Our Bones

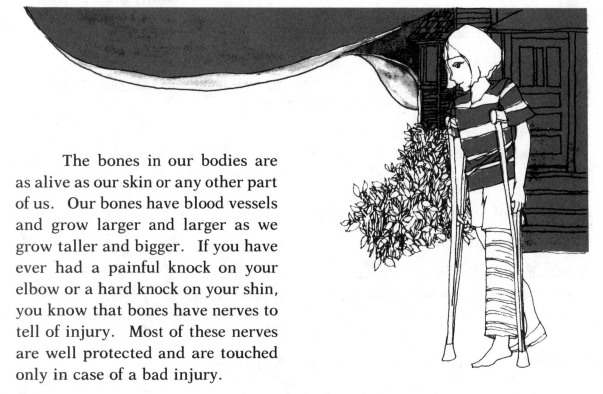

The bones in our bodies are as alive as our skin or any other part of us. Our bones have blood vessels and grow larger and larger as we grow taller and bigger. If you have ever had a painful knock on your elbow or a hard knock on your shin, you know that bones have nerves to tell of injury. Most of these nerves are well protected and are touched only in case of a bad injury.

Have you ever observed that older people break bones more easily than children do? As people grow older, their bones contain more mineral material. They become more brittle. For this reason, a fall that would not injure a child or a young person might cause an older person to break a bone.

If properly set, the broken bone of a young person will heal completely. This usually takes only 6 to 8 weeks. In a few months, the bone is usually as strong as it was before it was broken.

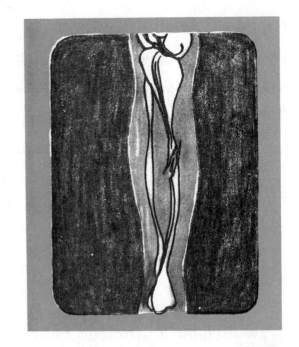

E-6 Testing Yourself

Draw a line under each right answer or fill in each blank.

1. Although not stated in the article, you can tell that

     a. bones cannot be badly injured.   b. bones form the body's frame.

            c. nerves are not easily damaged.

2. This article as a whole is about

     a. setting broken bones.   c. living body parts called bones.

     b. nerves and blood vessels.   d. mineral matter in bones.

3. The word **it** in the last sentence refers to _____ .

4. Nerves are poorly protected.   Yes   No   Does not say

5. Which two of these sentences are not true?

     a. Young bones usually heal quickly.   c. Broken bones can heal.

     b. Bones cannot break.   d. Bones have no nerves.

          e. Broken bones usually must be set to heal properly.

6. What word in the first paragraph, last sentence, means **come against?**

_____

Getting Ready to Read

SAY AND KNOW

arithmetic
related
opposites
sum
master
adding
subtracting
multiplying
dividing

Draw a line under each right answer or fill in the blank.

1. **Putting together** means   subtracting   sum   <u>adding</u>.

2. **Connected** means   opposite   related   multiplying.

3. **Completely different things** are   masters   opposites   sums.

4. **To become skillful at** means to   sum   master   divide.

5. **The answer in addition** is the   opposite   sum   master.

6. **The study of numbers** is called _____.

E-7   Related Arithmetic Facts

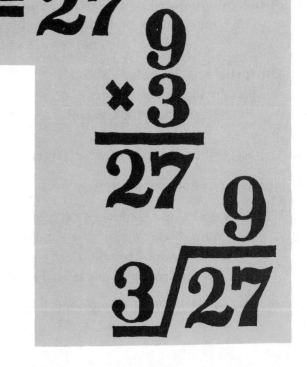

In adding 9 and 2, we get an answer of 11. In subtracting 2 from 11, we get an answer of 9. Adding and subtracting can be described as opposites. Each fact used in adding is related to one used in subtracting. After you have mastered 100 addition facts, it is easy for you to learn 100 subtraction facts.

Multiplying is a short or quick way of adding. If you add 9 and 9 and 9, you get the sum of 27.

96

After you learn the multiplication facts, it is shorter and quicker to multiply 9 by 3 in order to get the same answer of 27.

Dividing is related to multiplying in much the same way that subtracting is related to adding. Dividing can be described as the opposite of multiplying. For example, 9 times 3 is 27; 27 divided by 9 equals 3. It is easy to learn the division facts once you can multiply.

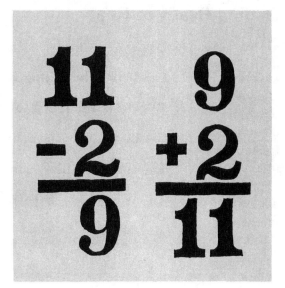

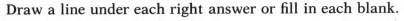

E-7   Testing Yourself

NUMBER RIGHT

Draw a line under each right answer or fill in each blank.

1. Although not stated in the article, you can tell that
   a. there are only 100 addition facts.   b. dividing is hard.
             c. arithmetic facts help us to work problems.

2. This article as a whole is about
   a. addition facts.   c. opposites in arithmetic.
   b. learning facts.   d. addition and subtraction.

3. The word **one** in the fourth sentence refers to _____.

4. Addition and subtraction facts are related.   Yes   No   Does not say

5. Which two of these sentences are not true?
   a. Multiplying is shorter than adding.   c. 9 times 3 is 11.
   b. Subtracting and dividing are the same.   d. 11 minus 2 is 9.
             e. Adding and subtracting are opposites.

6. What word in the last sentence means **things known to be true?**

Getting Ready to Read

kingdom
engage
outcome
command
trusted
mount
continue
achieve
messenger
loosened

Draw a line under each right answer or fill in the blank.

1. **Land ruled by a king** is a   **messenger**   **kingdom**   **mount.**

2. **To get on a horse** is to   **engage**   **continue**   **mount.**

3. **Get done** means   **achieve**   **continue**   **loosened.**

4. **The result** is the   **command**   **outcome**   **kingdom.**

5. **An order** is a   **trusted**   **command**   **outcome.**

6. It means **keep on.** _____

E-8   For the Want of a Nail . . .

Many years ago, the armies of two kingdoms were engaged in fighting a long war. Neither side was able to win. Finally, came the eve of a great battle that might decide the outcome of the war. One leader commanded a trusted messenger to ride all night. The messenger was to bring the rest of the army to the spot where the battle was to take place.

The army blacksmith told the rider that a nail was missing from one of the horse's shoes and that the

98

shoe would soon come loose. The messenger did not think the missing nail important. In a hurry to leave as quickly as possible, the messenger rode swiftly away.

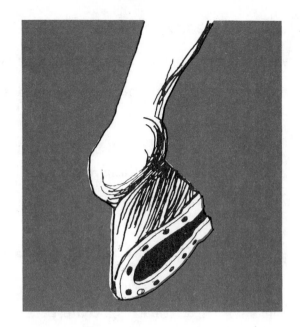

After a short time, the shoe loosened, and the horse became lame. They went slowly on. Finally, the horse was so lame that it could go no further. The messenger had to continue on foot. By the time the message was delivered, the battle was lost and the kingdom with it.

E-8 Testing Yourself

NUMBER RIGHT

Draw a line under each right answer or fill in each blank.

1. Although not stated in the article, you can tell that
    a. the messenger was cruel.   b. the blacksmith was wrong.
         c. small things can affect great things.

2. This article as a whole is about
    a. a lame horse.   c. a small mistake that lost a battle.
    b. a blacksmith.   d. a stupid messenger.

3. The word **it** in the last sentence refers to _____.

4. The messenger returned in time.   Yes   No   Does not say

5. Which two of these sentences are not true?
    a. The messenger was too slow.   c. The blacksmith was wrong.
    b. The messenger won the battle.   d. The horse became lame.
         e. The messenger did not give up.

6. What word in the first paragraph, third sentence, means **settle?**

Getting Ready to Read

economist

market

perfect

imperfect

competitive

product

competition

buyer

seller

different

Draw a line under each right answer or fill in the blank.

1. It means **one who studies the uses of money and goods.**

   market   buyer   economist

2. **Something without fault** is   competitive   imperfect   perfect.

3. **Something made** is called **a**   market   product   economist.

4. **People working against one another** may be

   imperfect   different   competitive.

5. **A place where goods are bought and sold** may be **a**

   market   product   competition.

6. It means **a contest** _____.

E-9   Money Matters

Economists are people who study the uses of money and the buying and selling of goods. Economists often talk about the "market." By market, they usually mean all the buying and selling of goods made over the world.

At one time, economists described this market as "perfect."

In a perfect market, a seller whose prices are too high will lose customers. One whose prices are too low will not make money. Economists believed that prices in a free market would be well balanced.

In the 1930s, however, an English economist named Joan Robinson studied the market in free countries. She found problems. She showed that sellers often raise prices above those of other sellers. They can do this because their products are different or because people believe that they are different. Makers or sellers can also set their own prices if no one else is selling the goods they make. They can sell the same thing for different prices in different places.

Robinson wrote a book about the way the market works in free countries. She called it *The Economics of Imperfect Competition*. She has helped us deal with the problems in an imperfect market.

E-9   Testing Yourself

Draw a line under each right answer or fill in each blank.

1. Although not stated in the article, you can tell that
   a. Joan Robinson changed the thinking of other economists.
   b. Joan Robinson wrote an important book.   c. prices do not change.

2. This article as a whole is about
   a. how the free market works.   c. buying goods.
   b. Joan Robinson's writing.   d. making money.

3. The word **they** in the third sentence refers to _____.

4. Joan Robinson has lived in the United States.   Yes   No   Does not say.

5. Which two of these sentences are not true?
   a. Joan Robinson is an important   c. All markets are perfect.
      economist.   d. Joan Robinson studied the
   b. Economists make and sell goods.   market.
              e. Prices in free markets are not always competitive.

6. What word in the second paragraph, fourth sentence, means **adjusted with equal**

   parts? _____

A Good Neighbor

In May of 1939, a steamship set sail from Hamburg, Germany. On it were more than 900 passengers, men, women, and children of all ages. They were Germans, but they had to leave Germany because its leaders at that time were taking cruel steps against Germans of the Jewish faith. The leaders were forcing the Jews and others out of their homes and jobs and into prison camps. The passengers on the *Saint Louis* were German Jews who knew that they had to leave Germany.

These people hoped to find temporary refuge in Cuba. They needed enough time to make plans for a new life. They had the necessary papers for the trip—passports and entry permits. When the ship set sail, they looked forward to the future even as they said goodbye to the past.

The captain of the *Saint Louis* was not Jewish. He was a German named Gustav Schroeder. For him and for everyone on his ship, this voyage turned out to be a test of kindness, courage, and love for one's neighbor. Before the *Saint Louis* even reached Cuba, laws permitting the entry of refugees had changed. When the ship arrived in Havana harbor, Cuban officials would not permit the passengers to land.

Can you imagine this ocean liner moored in a harbor, carrying passengers who feared that they might never begin the new life on which their hopes rested? These passengers had lost their homes in their own country. They might lose their lives if they went back. Here is how a newspaper reporter described the scene:

Late this afternoon the *Saint Louis* was surrounded by boats filled with relatives and friends of those on board. Police patrolled the liner's docks and forbade any except government officials to . . . step on the floating dock alongside the ship. Huge spotlights attached to the vessel's sides lighted the surrounding waters tonight. The *Saint Louis* passengers, many sobbing desperately, lined the rail and talked with those in the surrounding boats. . . .

For many days, Captain Schroeder had taken good care of his passengers. Most of them were by now sick with fear. He told Cuban officials that these desperate people might kill themselves before they would return to Germany. Schroeder's ship had been ordered to return at once. After it became clear that Cuba would not change its laws, the captain went back to sea. He kept the ship in the waters off the southern coast of the United States. He hoped that some other country might offer his passengers a home.

Germany thought of these refugees as enemies. Captain Schroeder was a German, but he would not desert them! While they were aboard his ship, they were in his charge. Their safety was in his hands.

After many days, a way was found to provide refuge for the passengers. They did not have to go back to Hamburg. They were received in four groups by England, France, Holland, and Belgium. That was in June 1939. This was just before World War II broke out in Europe.

Many years later, a movie was made about the voyage of the *Saint Louis*. Some of its passengers who had survived the war still remembered the kind captain who had been so courageous and a good neighbor to them all.

MY READING TIME _____ **(420 WORDS)**

Thinking It Over

1. According to this story, who are your neighbors?

2. The good neighbor in this story was a captain and a leader. In what ways can we be good neighbors?

3. Can you tell a story of someone who was a good neighbor?

Getting Ready to Read

dweller
western
beard
goddess
forehead
muscle
weak
tribe
scarce

Draw a line under each right answer or fill in the blank.

1. **The opposite of strong** is   **long**   **scarce**   **weak.**

2. **One who lives somewhere** is a   **tribe**   **dweller**   **goddess.**

3. **The front part of the head** is called the
     muscle   **forehead**   **beard.**

4. **Hair growing on the face** can be a   **tribe**   **beard**   **muscle.**

5. **Something rare** is   **weak**   **scarce**   **western.**

6. The Rocky Mountains are in _____ North America.

F-1   Unusual Tree-Dwellers

There are several interesting kinds of monkeys in western Africa. One of these is called the Diana monkey. Both male and female Diana monkeys have long tails and white pointed beards. On its forehead, each monkey has a white spot shaped like a new moon. Because the Roman moon goddess was named Diana, these monkeys are named Diana monkeys.

Many monkeys can hang by their tail and use it in jumping and in climbing. The Diana monkey cannot do this. The muscles in its tail are so weak that it does not seem to be useful for anything.

Diana monkeys live in the forests and are usually found in a

104

large group, sometimes called a tribe. They live high up in the trees most of the time and travel long distances through the treetops. They eat insects and birds' eggs. Sometimes, when food is scarce, they will even eat young birds.

Unfortunately, the Diana monkey is becoming scarce itself. The forests they live in are being destroyed, and unless something is done, they may die out.

F-1   Testing Yourself

NUMBER RIGHT

Draw a line under each right answer or fill in each blank.

1. Although not stated in the article, you can tell that
   a. Diana monkeys need tails.   b. Diana monkeys help one another.
            c. Diana monkeys can climb without using their tails.

2. This article a whole is about
   a. monkeys without tails.   c. Diana monkeys.
   b. tribes of monkeys.   d. western Africa.

3. The word **it** in the second paragraph, third sentence, refers to

   _____

4. Diana monkeys are named for the Roman goddess of the moon, Diana.

                              Yes   No   Does not say

5. Which two of these sentences are not true?
   a. The number of Diana monkeys is growing.   c. Only male monkeys have beards.
   b. Monkeys live in Africa.   d. Most monkeys have strong tails.
            e. Diana monkeys live mainly in the treetops.

6. What word in the first sentence means **worth attention**?

   _____

Getting Ready to Read

Draw a line under each right answer or fill in the blank.

pharaoh

reign

ancient

elaborate

archeologist

hieroglyphics

painstakingly

antechamber

mummy

casket

1. It means **outer room.**   casket   reign   antechamber

2. When people are very careful about how they do something, they do it _____   **painstakingly   elaborately   mummy.**

3. **Someone who studies objects people used long ago** is   **a mummy   a pharaoh   an archeologist.**

4. It is the **opposite of modern.**   **elaborate   ancient   hieroglyphic**

5. Long ago, an **Egyptian king** was called a   **mummy   pharaoh   casket.**

6. **It is a kind of picture writing.** _____

F-2   The 3,000-Year-Old Boy-King

Tutankhamen became Pharaoh of Egypt when he was only 9 years old. He did not reign long, however. He died when he was 18 or 19. Like all the pharaohs of ancient Egypt, Tutankhamen was buried in an elaborate tomb surrounded by beautiful objects.

The tomb was built under ground with secret passages and fake doorways designed to fool treasure hunters. That is why the tomb remained untouched for over 3,000 years, and Tutankhamen was all but forgotten.

In 1922, an archeologist named Howard Carter found the tomb. He had been searching for it for over ten years when one of his workers came upon a stone step under a hut. The step was the first of fifteen that led down to a sealed door. The hieroglyphics on the door told them that Tutankhamen lay within.

Slowly, painstakingly, Carter's team unsealed the door and made their way down a long passage to a second door. It opened onto a glittering world of jewels and gold of amazing beauty. This was only the beginning. The team found that the room was just an antechamber.

Even greater treasure lay in the burial chamber within, but it

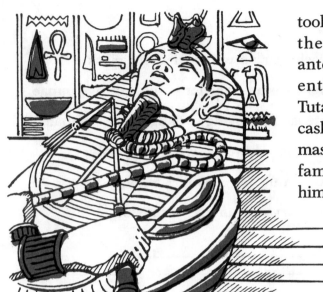

took Carter's team two years to open the heart of the tomb. After the anteroom was cleared, they finally entered the burial chamber. Tutankhamen's mummy lay in a gold casket. Over his head was a pure gold mask. Today the face of the mask is familiar to many people. We know him as King Tut, the boy-king.

F-2 Testing Yourself

NUMBER RIGHT

Draw a line under each right answer or fill in each blank.

1. While not directly stated, it can be reasoned from the article that
   a. Howard Carter did not expect to find the tomb.
   b. it is unusual for archeologists to find so many valuable objects in one tomb.
   c. There are many undiscovered Pharaoh tombs in Egypt.

2. This article as a whole is about
   a. Tutankhamen's tomb.   b. archeology.   c. Howard Carter.

3. The word **it** in paragraph four refers to _____.

4. King Tut was married when he was still a child.   Yes   No   Does not say

5. Which two sentences are not true?
   a. Tutankhamen's mummy was found in a pyramid.
   b. It took Howard Carter many years to locate the tomb.
   c. The archeologists cleared the anteroom after they inspected the burial chamber.
   d. Tutankhamen reigned for 9 or 10 years.
   e. Nobody had been inside the tomb for over 3,000 years.

6. What word in paragraph one means **things**? _____

Getting Ready to Read

SAY AND KNOW

annoying
wiggler
larvae
pupae
split
mosquito
bitten
transmit
dangerous
malaria
toxic

Draw a line under each right answer or fill in the blank.

1. **Something that wiggles** is a   **wiggler**   **mosquito**   **pupae.**

2. **The opposite of safe** is   **annoying**   **dangerous**   **pupae.**

3. **Something disturbing** is   **bitten**   **split**   **annoying.**

4. **To break open** is to   **transmit**   **split**   **malaria.**

5. **To pass along** is to   **larvae**   **annoy**   **transmit.**

6. It means **poisonous.** _____

F-3   An Annoying Insect

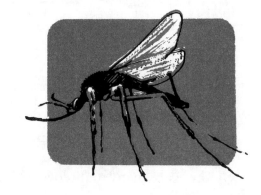

Did you ever look into a tin can or a rain barrel that has had water standing in it for some time? If so, you may have seen wigglers in the water. These wigglers are baby mosquitoes called larvae. Larvae shed their skins four times. Then they enter a new stage of life and are called pupae. After 2 or 3 days, the skin of the pupa splits, and out flies a full-grown mosquito.

Mosquitoes are very annoying insects. The female mosquito sucks the blood of human beings. When she does this, we say we have been bitten. Some kinds of mosquitoes carry diseases that they transmit from one person to another through bites. Yellow fever is the most dangerous of these diseases. Another dangerous illness carried and transmitted by mosquitoes is called malaria.

We can reduce the number of mosquitoes by draining swamps and other places where they breed. We can also spray these places with a thin layer of oil. The oil keeps air from the larvae and they die. Or we can kill mosquitoes in the areas where they live with toxic sprays.

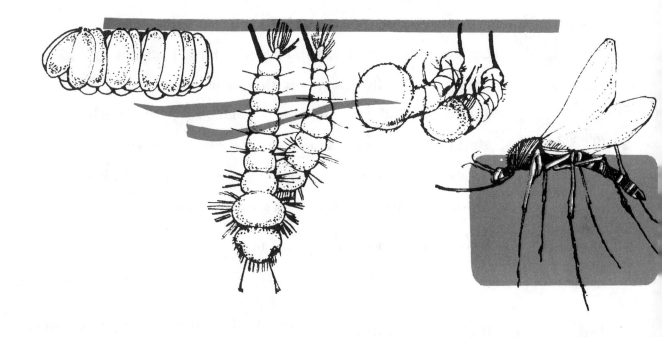

F-3 Testing Yourself

Draw a line under each right answer or fill in each blank.

1. Although not stated in the article, you can tell that
   - a. mosquitoes breed in still water.
   - b. all mosquitoes carry disease.
   - c. yellow fever is now easily cured.

2. This article as a whole is about
   - a. mosquitoes.
   - b. rain barrels.
   - c. the spread of measles.
   - d. draining swamps.

3. The word **they** in the fifth sentence refers to _____.

4. Mosquitoes are helpful insects.   Yes   No   Does not say

5. Which two of these sentences are not true?
   - a. Some mosquitoes carry malaria.
   - b. Mosquitoes are harmful.
   - c. We should help mosquitoes breed.
   - d. Pupae are full-grown mosquitoes.
   - e. Draining swamps helps to eliminate mosquitoes.

6. What word in the last paragraph, first sentence, means **removing water?**

Getting Ready to Read

SAY AND KNOW

population
cattle
produces
refining
industry
supplies
Spanish
independent
television
broadcast

Draw a line under each right answer or fill in the blank.

1. They are called **livestock.**   cattle   population   supplies

2. **The act of making** is   refining   producing   broadcasting.

3. **Making pure** means   supplying   television   refining.

4. **Not depending on others** is being   Spanish   refined   independent.

5. **Provides** means   supplies   broadcasts   produces.

6. **To send programs over the air** is to _____.

F-4   Bigger than Its Neighbors

Except for the state of Alaska, Texas is the largest of the American states in territory. It is also one of the largest of the states in population.

Texas is noted for its huge cattle ranches and for its many sheep. It also produces large crops of cotton, winter wheat, corn, and fruit. And in Texas, oil refining is a major industry. Texas supplies oil to the West, Midwest, and North.

Texas was a part of Spanish America when the first North American settlement was made there in 1821. For a time, Texas was a part of Mexico. In 1836, it became inde-

pendent, and in 1845, it became the twenty-eighth state of the United States.

If you were to visit Texas today, you would see many signs of its Spanish history. Many Texans speak Spanish. Many of the state's radio and television stations broadcast in Spanish. Texans have kept some of the beautiful, old Spanish churches in good repair. And you can read Texas's Spanish history in its place names. San Antonio, El Paso, Amarillo, and Laredo are all Texas cities.

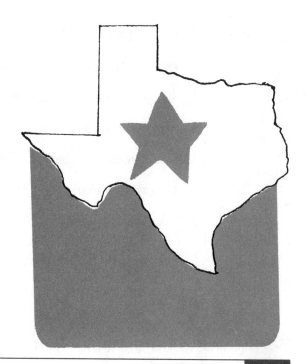

F-4 Testing Yourself

NUMBER RIGHT

Draw a line under each right answer or fill in each blank.

1. Although not stated in the article, you can tell that
    a. Texas is our largest state.   b. Texas is a rich state.
    c. Texas has large cotton and wheat crops.

2. This article as a whole is about
    a. an independent Texas.   c. raising cattle.
    b. oil in Texas.   d. one of our largest states.

3. The word **its** in the fourth paragraph, fifth sentence, refers to _____.

4. Texas was once a part of Mexico.   Yes   No   Does not say

5. Which two of these sentences are not true?
    a. Texas is smaller than Alaska.   c. Few people live in Texas.
    b. No Texans speak Spanish.   d. Texas produces oil.
    e. Texas was our twenty-eighth state.

6. What word in the second paragraph, first sentence, means **especially known?**

Getting Ready to Read

Draw a line under each right answer or fill in the blank.

waffle
obtain
syrup
hollow
tublike
vat
brief
collect
season
sap

1. **To get** means **to**   obtain   hollow   waffle.

2. **A time of year** is **a**   vat   tublike   season.

3. **Short** means   hollow   brief   vat.

4. **To gather** means **to**   vessel   collect   hollow.

5. **The juice of trees** is   vat   sap   waffle.

6. **A sweet, thick liquid** is called _____.

F-5   Sweets from Maple Trees

Have you ever eaten maple syrup on your pancakes or waffles? Maple syrup is obtained from maple trees, many of which grow in New England.

In the spring, when the sap begins to flow, farmers cut holes in the trunks of the maple trees. They put in plastic spouts and then run plastic tubing from tree to tree. The sap runs out through the spouts and into the tubing. It can then be collected in one place. Sometimes farmers also collect the sap the old-fashioned way. They put hollow pegs in the trees and hang buckets from them.

People pour the sap into a big, tublike vat and boil it down until it becomes syrup. It takes about 10.5 gallons (40 liters) of sap to make about .25 gallons (1 liter) of syrup.

Although the season for collecting sap is a brief one, enough sap is collected in the United States to make almost 2.5 million pounds of maple syrup each year. The syrup is then put into bottles and sold or made into maple sugar.

F-5 Testing Yourself   **NUMBER RIGHT**

Draw a line under each right answer or fill in each blank.

1. Although not stated in the article, you can tell that
   a. maple sap tastes sweet.   b. all maple trees grow in New England
       c. syrup is made each year in the United States.

2. This article as a whole is about
   a. maple trees.   c. making sugar.
   b. maple syrup.   d. boiling sap.

3. The word **one** in the last paragraph, first sentence, refers to

   _____.

4. Maple syrup is expensive.   Yes   No   Does not say

5. Which two of these sentences are not true?
   a. Sap flows in summer.   c. We get the syrup from trees.
   b. Maple trees have sap.   d. We get the sap only from trees.
       e. Much maple syrup is made each year in the United States.

6. What word in the second sentence means **gotten?** _____

Getting Ready to Read

Draw a line under each right answer or fill in the blank.

1. **One who knows much about some special things** is warnings   an expert   a citizen.

2. **To come into being** can mean to   **arise**   **conditions**   **expert.**

3. **To supply** means to   **arise**   **forecast**   **provide.**

4. **Telling beforehand** is   **predicting**   **expert**   **conditions.**

5. **A flyer** is   **an aviator**   **a weather expert**   **a citizen.**

6. **A member of a state or nation** is a _____.

F-6   Predicting Weather

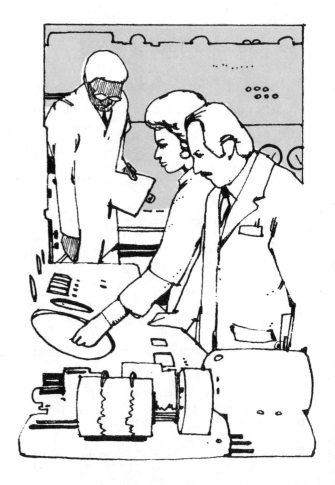

The United States government provides many services for its citizens. One of these is forecasting the weather. From facts collected each day, a weather expert can usually tell what weather conditions will follow in the next day or two. Because new conditions may arise quickly, mistakes are sometimes made. Over a long period of time, however, weather reports tend to be correct.

Weather warnings often save crops. They may even save lives. For example, the report of a coming frost will send fruit growers into their orchards to light fires. They hope that the heat will keep the fruit

114

from harm. Farmers will not spray trees or cut hay if they learn that rain is on the way. Aviators, fishers, and sailors check the latest weather reports before starting their trips. Thousands of other people plan their trips and even their daily clothing according to the reports of the weather experts.

As you can see, the weather is important to all of us. Forecasting weather is a very helpful service.

F-6 Testing Yourself

Draw a line under each right answer or fill in each blank.

1. Although not stated in the article, you can tell that
    a. weather affects people.   b. weather is usually bad.
        c. weather can be changed by people.

2. This article as a whole is about
    a. weather and predicting weather.   c. becoming a sailor.
    b. ways of predicting weather.   d. the result of frost.

3. The word **their** in the second paragraph, third sentence, refers to

                                 _____.

4. Frost may harm fruit.   Yes   No   Does not say

5. Which two of these sentences are not true?
    a. Weather experts make no   c. Weather reports are mostly
       mistakes.   wrong.
    b. Weather warnings help us.   d. Weather can change quickly.
        e. Aviators must know about the weather.

6. What word in the second paragraph, last sentence, means **accounts or descrip-**

tions of? _____

Getting Ready to Read

SAY AND KNOW

comma
separate
group
easier
farthest
unit
period
using
figure
population

Draw a line under each right answer or fill in the blank.

1. **Making use of** means   **separate**   **farthest**   **using.**

2. One mark of **punctuation** is a   **group**   **comma**   **unit.**

3. **The opposite of closest** is   **period**   **unit**   **farthest.**

4. **More easily** means   **period**   **figure**   **easier.**

5. **To take apart** is to   **unit**   **separate**   **population.**

6. A number of things together form a _____.

F-7   Reading and Writing Big Numbers

One year in the United States, one hundred fifteen million, four hundred fifty-six thousand, eight hundred seventy-two bushels of apples were raised. This big number may be written in figures as 115,456,872. Notice that we use commas to separate this big number into groups of three figures each. These groups are called periods. Using commas to break such a large number into smaller groups makes the number easier to read.

If we begin reading at the right, the name of the first period, or group of numbers, is *units* or *ones*. The next group is called *thousands*. The third group is

called *millions*. The period farthest to the left may have one, two, or three figures. The numbers within each period, starting from the number farthest to the right, are called *ones, tens, and hundreds.*

In 1990, the population of California was 29,839,250. Can you read this number? Can you right it in words only? The sun is about 92,500,000 miles (152,100,00 kilometers) from Earth. Can you read these big numbers? Can you write them in words only?

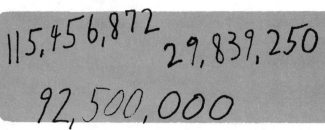

115,456,872   29,839,250

92,500,000

F-7   Testing Yourself

NUMBER RIGHT

Draw a line under each right answer or fill in each blank.

1. Although not stated in the article, you can tell that
   a. we all know how to use big numbers.   b. the sun is not large.
      c. there are two ways to write big numbers.

2. This article as a whole is about
   a. California.   c. big numbers.
   b. raising apples.   d. reading population numbers.

3. The word **it** in the last paragraph, third sentence, refers to

   _____.

4. The United States raises more apples than Canada.   Yes   No   Does not say

5. Which two of these sentences are not true?
   a. Commas separate big numbers.   c. Number groups are periods.
   b. You can divide numbers into groups.   d. Numbers are all small.
      e. In 1970, California's population was less than 12 million.

6. What word in the first sentence means **grown?** _____

Getting Ready to Read

Hawaiian
devised
manage
wove
probably
foundered
drown
image
adventure

Draw a line under each right answer or fill in the blank.

1. **To be able to do** is to   **founder   manage   drown.**

2. **Figured out** means   **imagined   devised   wove.**

3. **To imagine** is to   **plan   picture in your mind   devise.**

4. **Tying to** means   **fastening   devising   foundering.**

5. When a boat sinks it   **images   manages   founders.**

6. Something likely to be true is ———————————— true.

F-8   Sailing Adventures

Many stories are told about sailing and the sea. One story tells of a Hawaiian boy who wished to cross the water from one island to another. He did not know how to manage a canoe alone, but he devised a way.

He got two poles. Then he wove long leaves into a mat. He fastened the mat to the poles. He put them into the canoe to make the first sailboat.

That story is probably a folktale. But we have records of many true sailing adventures. For example, an Englishwoman named Ann Davison dreamed of sailing across the Atlantic Ocean. In 1948, she and her husband set sail, but the boat foundered and her husband drowned. Four years later, Ann Davison sailed alone from England to the United States. Her boat was only 23 feet (6.9 meters) long.

Other people have sailed the Atlantic in larger, faster boats. Sir Francis Chichester set a record in 1970 by crossing in 22 days.

Can you imagine sailing alone on the ocean for months? Most sailors choose less dangerous adventures. Still, sailors continue to set out on daring voyages every year.

F-8   Testing Yourself

NUMBER RIGHT

Draw a line under each right answer or fill in each blank.

1. Although not stated in the article, you can tell that
    a. the Hawaiian boy liked to swim.   b. sailboats are only for short trips.
              c. sailing is an adventurous sport.

2. This article as a whole is about
    a. the Hawaiian Islands.   c. sailboating adventures.
    b. a clever boy.   d. a woman who sailed the Atlantic.

3. The word **he** in the third sentence refers to _____.

4. Ann Davison sailed in a 23 foot boat.   Yes   No   Does not say

5. Which two of these sentences are not true?
    a. The Hawaiian boy made his canoe a sailboat.
    b. Records show that men and women have sailed the Atlantic alone.
    c. A sailing record was set in 1970.
    d. We have records of the Hawaiian boy's deed.
    e. No one has sailed the Atlantic alone.

6. What word in the third paragraph, fourth sentence, means **sank?**

_____

Getting Ready to Read

SAY AND KNOW

prime

minister

produce

product

politics

leadership

elections

public

office

Draw a line under each right answer or fill in the blank.

1. The top officer in some governments is called a

    minister   product   **prime minister.**

2. **To make something** means **to   produce   product   prime.**

3. **People taking part in government matters** are in

    public   politics   elections.

4. **People vote in   politics   parties   elections.**

5. **Something open to everyone** is   **prime   public   politics.**

6. **A person who is able to direct and guide others shows**

    _____.

F-9   An Island Leader

In 1960, people of the island of Sri Lanka chose a woman as Prime Minister, the top officer in the government.

Sri Lanka used to be called Ceylon. It is a beautiful island off the southeast coast of India. Island products are tea, rubber, coconut palms, and farm products.

Sirimavo Bandaranaike had been interested in politics for a long time. Her husband had been the Prime Minister of Sri Lanka until he was killed in 1959. At that time, Mrs. Bandaranaike became leader of the Freedom party. Under her leadership, the party won the most votes in the next elections.

Mrs. Bandaranaike had often said that she did not want public office. But she saw that the country looked upon her as a leader. She saw that members of the political parties were willing to work with her. Therefore, she accepted the post of Prime Minister. She became the first woman in modern times to hold such an office.

As Prime Minister, Mrs. Bandaranaike tried to bring more factories to this island of planters and crops. She knew that factories bring jobs. She also made education free for all children.

Sri Lanka

F-9 Testing Yourself

NUMBER RIGHT

Draw a line under each right answer or fill in each blank.

1. Although not stated in the article, you can tell that
   - a. Sri Lanka does not have many factories.
   - b. Mrs. Bandaranaike is a rich woman.
   - c. Mrs. Bandaranaike always wanted public office.

2. This article as a whole is about
   - a. farming in Sri Lanka.
   - b. coconut, rubber, and tea planting.
   - c. islands off the coast of India.
   - d. Sri Lanka and its Prime Minister.

3. The word **her** in the third paragraph refers to _____.

4. Mrs. Bandaranaike's husband is still alive.   Yes   No   Does not say

5. Which two of these sentences are not true?
   - a. Sri Lanka used to be called Ceylon.
   - b. Mrs. Bandaranaike was chosen Prime Minister in 1960.
   - c. Sri Lanka is not an island.
   - d. An education in Sri Lanka costs money.
   - e. Sri Lanka produces tea.

6. What two words in the first sentence mean **top government officer**?

_____   _____

The Children's March

Some of the children who marched with Mary Harris Jones from Pennsylvania to New York City were only 10 years old. Most were no more than 12 or 13. They carried knapsacks on their backs. Each knapsack contained a metal

cup and plate, knife and fork, and other things for daily use. One of the children had a drum. Another had a fife. Those two made up the children's band.

Were these children campers on a trip? That is what we would be likely to think today. But the facts about this march are very different. It took place in 1903, a time when our country had no strong laws against child labor. The children who formed Mary Jones's army were little workers. They worked in mills and textile factories. They

helped to make cloth, pack clothing, and tend machines. The work could be dangerous, especially when small children grew tired and careless. Many did grow tired. They had to awake before dawn to get to work in the early morning. They worked for as long as 10 or 12 hours a day. It was no wonder that some of them had broken or missing fingers from work accidents.

All the children called Mary Jones "Mother." So did their parents. Mary Jones was a labor-union organizer. She had begun her work years after she lost her husband, an iron worker, and her four children. They all died in a fever epidemic.

Those terrible losses made Mary Jones feel that she should spend her life helping other workers and their families lead healthier, happier lives. She believed that the way to do this was to organize workers into groups. She was convinced that a group, or union, could do for its members what individuals could not do for themselves. A group, for example, could force the passing of new laws.

The children who marched with Mother Jones were free to take this trip because they and their parents were on strike. They had all left their mill jobs in protest against low pay and bad conditions. The march began in the spring. And the children sometimes camped out along the way. But Mother Jones and her adult helpers made sure that the children had good food. They arranged for shelter when the weather was bad. People along the route helped.

Everywhere that she and her small army went, Mother Jones talked about the need for passing laws to keep little children from working in factories and mills. Everywhere, she showed listeners how small these children were for their ages. She explained that they seldom had time to play in the fresh air. They were always so tired that they fell asleep over their books.

Mother Jones's march was fun for the children. In New York, they went to the beach at Coney Island. Afterwards, a hotelkeeper served them the biggest and best breakfast that they had ever eaten. But the march was more than a holiday. Mother Jones and her children's army helped perform a great service for our country. They helped to bring about better laws against child labor.

MY READING TIME _____ **(420 WORDS)**

Thinking It Over

1. Why did Mother Jones spend her life helping workers?

2. How did the children help Mother Jones?

3. Why should we prevent, or regulate, child labor?

Getting Ready to Read

wholly
favorite
injured
plunder
pleasant
helpless
merchants
useful
sacred
langur

Draw a line under each right answer or fill in the blank.

1. **Hurt** means **helpless injured useful.**

2. **Completely** means **wholly favorite langur.**

3. **Of use** means **helpless useful sacred.**

4. **If something pleases,** it is **useful helpless pleasant.**

5. **To rob** is to **pleasant plunder useful.**

6. **The thing liked best** is the _____.

G-1 Sacred Monkeys

Many people in India regard langur monkeys as sacred. Because of this, in certain areas these long-tailed animals are never harmed. In such places, the monkeys soon become quite tame and have little or no fear of people.

Most langur monkeys live wholly on fruit and vegetables. They eat the fruit and vegetables growing in the fields around the villages. Sometimes passengers on trains carry nuts, bananas, and other foods so that they can feed the monkeys in the train stations.

At times, the sacred monkeys even go into village shops to choose their favorite foods. In areas where monkeys cannot be injured, they plunder at will. This is very pleasant for the monkeys, but not so pleasant for the helpless merchants!

In the past, these tame monkeys were sometimes useful. When a tiger troubled a village, the villagers set out on a tiger hunt. The monkeys would go along on the hunt, swinging through the trees, helping the hunters track the tiger.

G-1   Testing Yourself   **NUMBER RIGHT**

Draw a line under each right answer or fill in each blank.

1. Although not stated in the article, you can tell that
   a. all monkeys are tame.   b. langur monkeys do not eat meat.
      c. all Indians think that langur monkeys are sacred.

2. This article as a whole is about
   a. langur monkeys.   c. a tiger hunt.
   b. Indian merchants.   d. monkeys at train stations.

3. The word **they** in the third paragraph, second sentence, refers to

   _____.

4. Tigers eat langur monkeys.   Yes   No   Does not say

5. Which two of these sentences are not true?
   a. Some monkeys are tame.   c. Langur monkeys have been useful.
   b. People hunt tigers.   d. Langur monkeys have short tails.
      e. All Americans think langur monkeys are sacred.

6. What word in the last sentence means **follow?** _____

Getting Ready to Read

SAY AND KNOW

celebrate

dragon

evil

modern

contest

encourage

warrior

national

Draw a line under each right answer or fill in the blank.

1. **To do things in honor of a special day** is **to**

                                         celebrate   encourage   dragon.

2. **A fairy-tale animal with a long tail** is **a warrior   dragon   figure.**

3. **The opposite of good** is   **evil   national   modern.**

4. **A person who fights** is **a   warrior   national   firecracker.**

5. **A trial or competition** is **a   encourage   celebrate   contest.**

6. **When you want something done, you** ＿＿＿＿＿＿ **it.**

G-2   Celebrations of Two Lands

People who came to the United States from China brought with them some Chinese ways of life. For example, many Chinese Americans still celebrate the Chinese New Year by parading and dancing in the streets. This holiday comes a few weeks after January 1. Celebrators carry large paper ani-

mals that give the name of the year. For the Chinese Year of the Dragon, the paper is shaped like a dragon.

Strangely enough, today more of these parades may be seen here than in China. In old China, dragon dancing was thought to keep away evil spirits. The leaders of modern China do not encourage dragon dancing.

Parades are not the only way Chinese Americans have celebrated their love of two lands. A young woman born in California of Chinese parents found another way. She wrote a book that was both about America and about the stories of China her mother had told her. She called her book *The Woman Warrior,* after a Chinese story about a brave female soldier. In a contest with books by many famous writers, this book by Maxine Hong Kingston won the National Book Award.

G-2   Testing Yourself

Draw a line under each right answer or fill in each blank.

1. Although not stated in the article, you can tell that
      a. dragon dancing is seen all over modern China.
      b. Chinese New Year's celebrations are lively.
      c. all Chinese believe in evil spirits.

2. This article as a whole is about
      a. China.
      b. New Year's parades.
      c. holidays and parades.
      d. loving two different ways of life.

3. The word **she** in the third paragraph, third sentence, refers to

      _____.

4. The New Year is no longer celebrated in China.   Yes   No   Does not say

5. Which two of these sentences are not true?
      a. Many Chinese who have come to America celebrate the Chinese New Year.
      b. A book by a Chinese American woman won a prize.
      c. Paper dragons are no longer made anywhere.
      d. Modern China is not the same as old China.
      e. All Chinese love dragon dancing.

6. The word in the last sentence of paragraph two that means **to support or inspire** is

      _____.

127

Getting Ready to Read

cotton
boll weevil
destroys
native
destructive
silky
fibers
thrive
harmful
depended
livelihood
steadier
prosperity

Draw a line under each right answer or fill in the blank.

1. **Something that does damage is**   steadier   harmful   silky.

2. **Threadlike pieces of material are**   fibers   natives   silky.

3. **Relied on means**   depended   destroyed   thrived.

4. **Means of living is called**   prosperity   livelihood   native.

5. **Something destructive is something that**

                                    thrives   depends   destroys.

6. **Success or good fortune means** _____.

G-3   An Enemy of Cotton

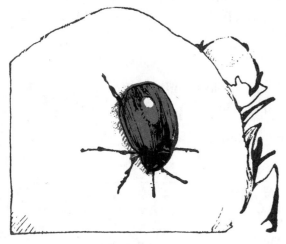

The boll weevil, an insect that destroys cotton plants, first found its way to the United States in 1892. Native to Central America, the destructive weevil had spread through Mexico and over the border into Texas. From there, it quickly spread to every state in which cotton was grown.

Boll weevils eat the silky fibers inside the seed pods of cotton plants. They also eat the buds of cotton flowers. Four or five times during a single season, female weevils lay their eggs inside the cotton buds. When the eggs hatch, the small insects feed on the insides of the buds.

The government has a plan to get rid of the boll weevil by spraying a powerful poison over cotton fields. But this spraying is believed to also kill spiders and other useful insects. There are no easy answers to the problem of garden pests.

Although boll weevils have been a big problem, they have also caused some good. Many farmers who had depended on cotton alone for their livelihood were forced to raise other crops. By doing so, some of the farmers gained steadier incomes and greater prosperity.

G-3 Testing Yourself

Draw a line under each right answer or fill in each blank.

1. Although not stated in the article, you can tell that

      a. cotton grows in Central America.   b. cotton flowers are white.

                c. boll weevils also eat wheat.

2. This article as a whole is about

      a. cotton.   c. the boll weevil.

      b. importing cotton.   d. a native of Mexico.

3. The word **they** in the second paragraph, second sentence, refers to

      _____ _____.

4. Boll weevils harm cotton.   Yes   No   Does not say

5. Which two of these sentences are not true?

      a. Boll weevils are harmful.   c. Boll weevils are plants.

      b. Boll weevils eat cotton.   d. Boll weevils lay eggs.

          e. Boll weevils are found only in the United States.

6. What word in the last sentence means **more regular?** _____

Getting Ready to Read

SAY AND KNOW

flowing
channels
rushing
carved
region
bay
map
Potomac
Susquehanna
Chesapeake

Draw a line under each right answer or fill in the blank.

1. **A flat drawing of the earth is a**   bay   map   region.

2. **Cut may mean**   **rushing**   **channels**   **carved.**

3. **Area means**   **bay**   **region**   **Chesapeake.**

4. **A part of the sea that extends into the land is a** **Susquehanna**   **channel**   **bay.**

5. **Moving with speed and force is**   **flowing**   **rushing**   **map.**

6. Washington, D.C., is located on the _____ River.

G-4   Drowned Rivers

Have you ever heard of a drowned river? You may be surprised to learn that the rivers flowing into Chesapeake Bay are called

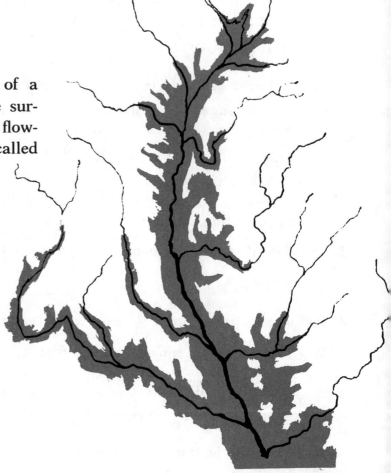

Chesapeake Bay

drowned rivers. The places at which these rivers enter the bay are not their real mouths. Their channels extend for a long distance under the waters of the bay.

Many thousands of years ago, what is now Chesapeake Bay was land. Rushing streams wore away the land as they carved out the valleys. For some reason, the land in this area sank below the level of the sea, and the water came up over the land to form the bay.

Suppose you could remove the water from Chesapeake Bay. Then you would be able to map the region, which includes parts of Pennsylvania, Maryland, and Virginia. You could see that the Susquehanna River is really the main stream of a river system. You would see where the Potomac and James rivers run into it. You would see that the lower parts of these rivers are covered by water or are drowned.

G-4   Testing Yourself

NUMBER RIGHT

Draw a line under each right answer or fill in each blank.

1. Although not stated in the article, you can tell that
    a. rivers change their channels.   b. rivers are wide and deep.
    c. land surface may change over many years' time.

2. This article as a whole is about
    a. three rivers under a bay.   c. the Susquehanna River.
    b. Chesapeake Bay.   d. a mountain system.

3. The word **they** in the second paragraph, second sentence, refers to

_____.

4. Drowned rivers are under water.   Yes   No   Does not say

5. Which two of these sentences are not true?
    a. Once Chesapeake Bay was land.   c. The James is a drowned river.
    b. Water can wear away land.   d. The whole Potomac is drowned.
    e. The James is the main stream of a river system.

6. What word in the second sentence means **running like water?**

_____

Getting Ready to Read

oleomargarine
margarine
homemade
aside
salted
factories
labor
substitutes
cottonseed
flavor

Draw a line under each right answer or fill in the blank.

1. It means **taste.**　　margarine　　salted　　flavor

2. **Made in the home** means　　factories　　homemade　　labor.

3. **Things used in place of other things** are
　　　　　　　　　　　　　　　　substitutes　　cottonseed　　factories.

4. **Work** means　　factories　　labor　　aside.

5. It is **used in place of butter.**　　homemade　　salted　　oleomargarine

6. Something with salt added has been _____.

G-5　Butter and Margarine

No one knows when or by whom butter was first made. We know that it has been used for several thousand years.

In the case of homemade butter, the cream is taken from the milk and set aside to sour. It is then churned until bits of fat come together. The lumps of fat are worked together and salted. The butter is then ready to be eaten or prepared for sale. Years ago, butter was made in the home. Churning butter by hand in a wooden container was hard work. Today, most of the butter sold is made in factories with machinery that saves labor in the churning.

132

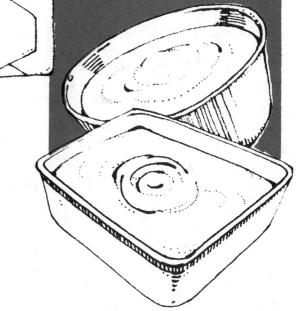

In recent years, butter substitutes such as oleomargarine have come into use. Oleomargarine was first made in France many years ago from oleo oil that came from beef fat. Most margarine today consists largely of cottonseed oil and soybean oil. Both kinds of oil are churned in milk to give them a flavor similar to butter.

G-5 Testing Yourself

Draw a line under each right answer or fill in each blank.

1. Although not stated in the article, you can tell that

      a. butter and margarine are the same.   b. butter is costly.

          c. cottonseed oil itself does not taste like butter.

2. This article as a whole is about

      a. the development of butter.   c. churning butter.

      b. butter and butter substitutes.   d. making butter at home.

3. The word **it** in the second paragraph, second sentence, refers to

      _____.

4. Oleomargarine is made from oil.   Yes   No   Does not say

5. Which two of these sentences are not true?

      a. Oleo was first made in France.   c. There is no fat in butter.

      b. Margarine substitutes for butter.   d. Margarine is not churned.

          e. Butter has been in use for many years.

6. What word in the last sentence means **beaten?** _____

Getting Ready to Read

SAY AND KNOW

particular
motion
forward
thus
compare
exactly
tides
seldom
stalk
undulating

Draw a line under each right answer or fill in the blank.

1. **Waving up and down** is   thus   undulating   seldom.

2. **Just so** means   **exactly**   **motion**   **tides.**

3. **Change of position or place** is called   **motion**   **tides**   **forward.**

4. **The opposite of backward** is   **thus**   **forward**   **seldom.**

5. **A thing apart from others** is   **compare**   **particular**   **stalk.**

6. **To see how things are alike and how they differ** means **to**

_____.

G-6   Movement of Ocean Water

Have you ever watched waves undulating in the ocean? Perhaps you have thought that the water in each wave had traveled for miles. Really, the water in each wave moves only a short distance, and in any particular part of the ocean, the water changes very little. Most of the motion of ocean water is up and down. The forward motion in one drop of water is given to the next drop and by this drop to the next one. Thus, the waves move over great distances, but the water itself goes a very short distance.

The movement of ocean waves can be compared with the waves caused by the wind in a field of grain. You can see the waves move across the field. But when a wave has passed, each stalk of grain is exactly where it was before the wave started.

The ocean water is always moving. The tides are coming in and going out. Storms come and go. But most of the water, except in the case of the ocean currents, seldom gets far from its regular place.

G-6   Testing Yourself

NUMBER RIGHT

Draw a line under each right answer or fill in each blank.

1. Although not stated in the article, you can tell that

    a. ocean waves are large.   b. ocean water is salty.

    c. things do not always act as they appear to act.

2. This article as a whole is about

    a. waves breaking on shore.   c. ocean water and beaches.

    b. the way ocean water moves.   d. ocean currents.

3. The word **it** in the second paragraph, last sentence, refers to

    _____.

4. Each drop of ocean water moves little in distance.   Yes   No   Does not say

5. Which two of the following sentences are not true?

    a. Ocean water moves up and down.   c. Water in waves travels far.

    b. Water in waves travels little.   d. Waves roll in the ocean.

    e. Water in ocean currents does not move far.

6. What word in the last sentence means **usual?** _____

135

Getting Ready to Read

Draw a line under each right answer or fill in the blank.

check

columns

opposite

addition

multiply

divisor

reverse

reversal

subtraction

1. **Things following one another in an upright line** make a
   column   reversal   divisor.

2. **Proving right by comparing** is   opposite   checking   divisor.

3. **As different as can be** means   opposite   columns   check.

4. **Turn backward** means   opposite   reverse   subtract.

5. **A number by which another is divided** is a
   divisor   reversal   multiply.

6. **When you take one number from another it is** _____.

G-7   Checking Arithmetic Answers

$$
\begin{array}{r}
13{,}564 \\
+\ 7{,}901 \\
\hline
21{,}465
\end{array}
\qquad
\begin{array}{r}
846 \\
-\ 291 \\
\hline
555
\end{array}
\qquad
\begin{array}{r}
2{,}000 \\
12\overline{)24{,}000}
\end{array}
$$

$$
\begin{array}{r}
21{,}465 \\
-\ 7{,}901 \\
\hline
13{,}564
\end{array}
\qquad
\begin{array}{r}
555 \\
+\ 291 \\
\hline
846
\end{array}
\qquad
\begin{array}{r}
2{,}000 \\
\times\ 12 \\
\hline
4000 \\
2000 \\
\hline
24{,}000
\end{array}
$$

Suppose you want to make sure that your answer in an addition problem is correct. How do you check to find out? First, you add by going up or down the column or columns. To check, you add by going in the opposite direction. If you add only two numbers, using subtraction to check your answer is also a good method.

To check your answer in subtraction, you add it to the smaller of the two numbers. If by adding these two numbers you get the same number as the original, larger number, your answer is correct.

To check your answer when you divide one number by another, you multiply the divisor by your answer. If your result is the number you divided, your answer is correct.

You see that when you subtract or divide, you check your answer by doing the reverse. If you are adding more than two numbers, then such a reversal is not a good, quick way to check answers.

G-7 Testing Yourself

NUMBER RIGHT

Draw a line under each right answer or fill in each blank.

1. Although not stated in the article, you can tell that
    a. adding is difficult.   b. adding and subtracting are alike.
      c. you cannot check all arithmetic problems the same way.

2. This article as a whole is about
    a. arithmetic.   c. subtraction.
    b. addition.   d. multiplication and division.

3. The word **it** in the second paragraph, first sentence, refers to

                                            _____.

4. Subtraction may be checked by adding.   Yes   No   Does not say

5. Which two of these sentences are not true?
    a. You can check arithmetic.   c. The reverse of multiplying is adding.
    b. Answers are always right.   d. The divisor is a number.
      e. Some addition may be checked by subtracting.

6. What word in the first sentence means **right?** _____

Getting Ready to Read

SAY AND KNOW

aviation

record

propeller

aviator

jet

average

speed

Draw a line under each right answer or fill in the blank.

1. This person flies an airplane. **an aviator** **a jet** **a propeller**

2. **Air travel** is called **jet** **Air Force** **aviation.**

3. **Motor-driven airplane blades** are called
                                                                jets **propellers** **aviators.**

4. **Rate of travel** is **record** **speed** **jet.**

5. The fastest plane is a _____ plane.

G-8 Racing in the Sky

As new kinds of planes are built, new aviation records are set. In California in 1951, Jacqueline Cochran flew a propeller plane more than 450 miles (725.05 kilometers) an hour. But in 1964, she beat that record. She flew a jet plane over

California at a speed of 1,400 miles (2,252.6 kilometers) an hour.

Only a year after Jacqueline Cochran's 1964 flight, her record was broken. Aviators R. L. Stephens and Darnel Andre flew 2,000 miles (3,218 kilometers) an hour over Andrews Air Force Base in California. Their plane was a jet.

The record right now is 2193 miles (3,529 kilometers) an hour. It was set in 1976 by Elton W. Soersz, at Beale Air Force Base in California.

Speed records are set on round-the-world flights, too. In 1986, Dick Rubin and Jeanne Yeager flew around the world without landing. Their average speed for the flight was 116 miles (186 kilometers) per hour.

G-8 Testing Yourself

Draw a line under each right answer or fill in each blank.

1. Although not stated in the article, you can tell that
   - a. jets have no motors.
   - b. Americans flew the first jet.
   - c. jets fly faster than propeller planes.

2. This article as a whole is about
   - a. aviators.
   - b. air speed records.
   - c. flying jet planes.
   - d. flying from California.

3. The word **she** in the first paragraph, third sentence, refers to

   _____.

4. People flew jets in 1957.   Yes   No   Does not say

5. Which two of these sentences are not true?
   - a. Jets can travel 2,000 miles an hour.
   - b. Propeller planes can fly long distances.
   - c. It is possible to fly all the way around the world without landing.
   - d. Aviation has not advanced since 1951.
   - e. No propeller plane can fly 400 miles an hour.

6. A person who flies at a new speed sets a _____.

Getting Ready to Read

observe

observing

social

group

scientist

anthropologist

history

pacific

Draw a line under each right answer or fill in the blank.

1. **More than one** is a   **history   group   social.**

2. **To watch** is to   **history   observe   social.**

3. **A number of people living together** forms a
                                   history   social group   island.

4. **A person who observes and studies a body of facts or truths** is
                          a scientist   an anthropologist   a history.

5. **A record of human past** is   **social   history   observing.**

6. **Someone who studies the history of people and their works** is an

_____ .

G-9   A Woman Pioneer

It was not strange that young Margaret Mead liked to observe people. Her mother was a social scientist. She studied the lives of people who came to the United States from other countries. Margaret's grandmother was a teacher.

When Margaret Mead grew up, she made observing people her lifework. She became an anthropologist. An anthropologist is a person who studies women and men and their works.

Most anthropologists had studied the history of early people by digging up old tools and bones. From these, they learned what early life must have been like. Margaret Mead did something different. She went to the Pacific islands. She lived there among people whose lives had changed little in hundreds of years.

Margaret Mead learned that people in different social groups behave in different ways. In the islands, she found groups in which women worked and men cared for children. She found groups in which women, not men, were fighters. She found groups in which no one fought.

Margaret Mead's habit of observing people helped to make her one of the top anthropologists in the world.

G-9   Testing Yourself

Draw a line under each right answer or fill in each blank.

1. Although not stated in the article, you can tell that
   a. Margaret Mead became rich.
   b. Margaret Mead found new ways to study people.
   c. Margaret Mead did not go to college.

2. This article as a whole is about
   a. Pacific islands.   c. an American woman scientist.
   b. anthropology.   d. early human history.

3. The word **she** in the third sentence refers to _____.

4. Margaret Mead learned that not all groups of people live in the same ways.

                                    Yes   No   Does not say

5. Which two of these sentences are not true?
   a. Margaret Mead was a pioneer in her work.
   b. Margaret Mead lived in the Pacific islands.
   c. Margaret Mead lived long ago.
   d. Margaret Mead studied early people by digging up their bones and tools.
   e. Margaret Mead became an important anthropologist.

6. What word in the third paragraph, first sentence, means a **person who studies**

   people and their works? _____.

The Bugler and the Bowman

Long ago, two men traveled through a lonely part of the country. One man was a brave soldier who had often gone to battle against the enemies of the country. The soldier carried a strong bow and a quiver full of arrows. The other man was younger. He carried only a bugle. This bugler had often called the soldiers to battle with his music, but he himself had never fought in one.

"What should you do," mocked the proud soldier, "if robbers were to attack us? I have my bow and arrows, but you have no weapon with which to defend yourself."

"It is true that I carry no weapon of war," answered the youth. "But with my music I can warn the soldiers that enemies are near. With my bugle I can send them messages."

"Music, indeed!" cried the soldier. "Give me my strong bow and swift arrows when there is danger near!"

By and by, the travelers came to a dense wood. Suddenly, robbers set upon them. Although the soldier fought bravely, he was soon wounded. Because the bugler had nothing with which to defend himself, the robbers did not hurt him in any way.

After supper, the band of robbers gathered about their great fire to sing and tell tales. The bugler stepped up to the robber captain. "I can play music for you, if you like," he said, hoping for the chance.

"Play war music for us," cried the captain. "Stir us for fighting!"

The bugler played a stirring song of war. Then he played a marching tune. Finally, the youth blew a loud, clear call to arms that would warn his country's soldiers that enemies were near. The robbers thought that this call was just a part of the music.

In the castle, far beyond the forest, one of the guards heard the call. "That is our bugler warning us that an enemy is at hand," cried the guard. "To arms! To arms!" A party of soldiers set off at once for the place from which the bugle had sounded. Surprising the robbers, the soldiers caught them all and set free the bugler and the wounded soldier.

Later that night, when they lay down to rest, the soldier said to his companion, "I was wrong, my young friend. A soldier must learn to fight with his head as well as with his hands. Weapons may fail, and then even a bugle may help in a way that a sword or a bow could not."

MY READING TIME _____ **(420 WORDS)**

Thinking It Over

1. Why didn't the bugler blow his call to arms as soon as he and the bowman were captured?

2. What did the bowman learn from the bugler?

3. What do you think the bugler might have learned from the bowman?

143

Getting Ready to Read

flick

surprising

feat

unable

beyond

sticky

helpful

sight

Draw a line under each right answer or fill in the blank.

1. **Something to see** is a   **flick**   **sight**   **feat.**

2. **A quick movement** is a   **beyond**   **feat**   **flick.**

3. **Not to be able** is to be   **sticky**   **beyond**   **unable.**

4. **The opposite of harmful** is   **helpful**   **sticky**   **surprising.**

5. **A great deed** is a   **feat**   **sight**   **flick.**

6. **Something that is not expected** is _____.

H-1 Pretty Tricky

Toads are common animals that can be found easily if we look for them. Have you ever seen a toad flick out its tongue and catch an insect several inches from its mouth? This is indeed a surprising sight. The toad can perform this unusual feat because its tongue is fastened in the front of its mouth. The free end lies farther back.

Our own tongues are fastened at the back. Most animals also have their tongues fixed at the back. Because of this, they are unable to stick their tongues out more than a short distance beyond their lips.

At the end of a toad's tongue, there is a sticky substance. When the tongue touches an insect, it curls about the bug. The sticky substance holds the insect tight while the toad pulls its tongue back into its mouth. In this way, toads can catch and eat a great many insects in a single day.

Toads are very helpful to farmers. If you have a garden, watch a toad catch insects. Be sure not to hurt it, for it helps you care for your plants.

H-1   Testing Yourself

NUMBER RIGHT

Draw a line under each right answer or fill in each blank.

1. Although not stated in the article, you can tell that
   - a. toads eat plants.
   - b. farmers should not kill toads.
   - c. toads eat mostly flies and mosquitoes.

2. This article as a whole is about
   - a. tongues.
   - b. toads.
   - c. farmers and insects.
   - d. eating toads.

3. The word **they** in the second paragraph, third sentence, refers to

   _____.

4. Toads are green.   Yes   No   Does not say

5. Which two of these sentences are not true?
   - a. Toads eat many insects.
   - b. People have tongues.
   - c. Toads have two tongues.
   - d. Toads can catch insects.
   - e. Toads' tongues are fastened at the back.

6. What word in the second sentence means **strike lightly and suddenly?**

   _____

Getting Ready to Read

Draw a line under each right answer or fill in the blank.

1. **Liking** means **being**   **fond of**   **accustomed to**   **grown in.**

2. Another word for **territories** or **areas** is   **oases**   **Arabs**   **regions.**

3. **A number of different kinds** means a   **spit**   **variety**   **oasis.**

4. **The condition of the weather in a place** is its

   climate   **desert**   **region.**

5. It means **in the habit of.** _____

H-2   Desert Food

Do you like to eat meat roasted on a barbecue? People in the desert regions of Arab countries have cooked this way for thousands of years. The meat Arabs eat comes from animals that live in the desert. They eat hares and lizards and a rodent called kangaroo rat because of its large feet and habit of hopping. Pieces of lamb roasted on a spit make up another favorite dish.

Many crops cannot be grown in dry desert lands. Therefore, the people do not have a variety of foods from which to choose. Dates, which can be raised in the oases, form an important part of the diets of desert people. They are fond of fresh dates dipped in butter and roasted over hot coals.

Desert dwellers are also fond

of the milk that they get from camels and goats. Because of the climate, the milk does not stay fresh for long. As a result, many people have grown accustomed to drinking sour milk. Cheese and butter are made from goats' and camels' milk.

Can you think of some foods eaten in this country that might seem strange to people of the desert?

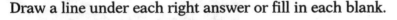

H-2 Testing Yourself

Draw a line under each right answer or fill in each blank.

1. Although not stated in the article, you can tell that
    a. dates taste sweet.   b. dates have tough skins.
       c. food is not usually imported into desert regions.

2. This article as a whole is about
    a. desert oases.   c. drinking sour milk.
    b. crops in the desert.   d. foods eaten by desert people.

3. The word **they** in the second paragraph, fourth sentence, refers to

_____.

4. Dates can be raised in oases.   Yes   No   Does not say

5. Which two of these sentences are not true?
    a. Desert people eat hares.   c. Many different crops grow in deserts.
    b. Camels do not give milk.   d. Cheese is made in Arab lands.
       e. Desert people eat roasted lamb.

6. What word in the second sentence means **nations**? _____

Getting Ready to Read

SAY AND KNOW

cicada
wormlike
nymph
bury
shed
relieved
sleeper
minute
emerge

Draw a line under each right answer or fill in the blank.

1. **Very small** means   **wormlike**   **minute**   **shed.**

2. **To come out** is to   **bury**   **shed**   **emerge.**

3. **To get rid of** is to   **shed**   **cicada**   **sleeper.**

4. **One who sleeps** is a   **nymph**   **sleeper**   **cicada.**

5. **Set free from worry** means   **minute**   **relieved**   **bury.**

6. **Something that is like a worm** is called _____.

H-3   The Long Sleep

Do you know that there is an insect that sleeps for 17 years? This insect is called the 17-year locust, but it is really a type of cicada.

The female makes tiny holes in the small branches of trees. In these small holes she lays her eggs. After a short time, the eggs hatch into minute, wormlike creatures called nymphs. The nymphs crawl down the trunks. They bury themselves in the ground at the bases of the trees. There they stay for 17 years. During this time, they grow slowly and live on the sap from the roots of trees.

After its 17-year sleep, the insect emerges from the ground. It

climbs onto a nearby tree. Soon it sheds its skin and flies out. It lives only six more weeks after this. Seventeen years seems a long time to prepare in order to live for 6 weeks.

Locusts live on growing plants, crops, and the leaves of trees and do them much injury. Farmers may feel relieved because these locusts live only 6 weeks.

148

ADULT CICADA

NYMPH

SHEDDING SKIN

H-3   Testing Yourself

Draw a line under each right answer or fill in each blank.

1. Although not stated in the article, you can tell that
      a. farmers do not like cicadas.   b. cicadas also eat other insects.
               c. locusts live only 6 weeks.

2. This article as a whole is about
      a. farmers.   c. what locusts eat.
      b. the cicada.   d. wormlike creatures.

3. The word **they** in the second paragraph, fifth sentence, refers to

                                        _____.

4. Nymphs sleep for 17 years.   Yes   No   Does not say

5. Which two of these sentences are not true?
      a. Nymphs bury themselves in the ground.   c. Locusts hurt trees.
      b. Nymphs are young cicadas.   d. Cicadas cannot fly.
               e. Locusts live only 17 days.

6. What word in the third paragraph, last sentence, means **get ready?**

                                          _____

Getting Ready to Read

SAY AND KNOW

official
dikes
dams
system
canals
drainage
windmills
pumps
electric
pleasure
herring
motorbike

Draw a line under each right answer or fill in the blank.

1. **A waterway dug across land** is a   canal   dam   dike.

2. It means **decided on by the proper bodies.**

    excess   official   electric

3. **Something people enjoy** gives   system   official   pleasure.

4. **A system of drying up** is called   canals   windmills   drainage.

5. **A kind of small fish** is a   pump   herring   system.

6. **A power-driven bicycle** is a _____.

H-4   Below the Sea

The Dutch sometimes say, "God created the world, but the Dutch made Holland." They mean that they have built their country in large part from land that is lower than the ocean. They know that they must fight the ocean to keep the land dry.

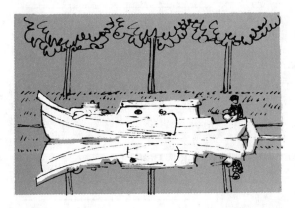

"The Netherlands," Holland's official name, means the lowlands. In order to live in these low-lying lands, the Dutch people have built high banks called dikes to keep out the water. They have also built large dams. And they have dug ditches, making a system of canals for draining the land. Then, too, the land behind the dikes must be kept free of too much rainwater. For this land drainage, the Dutch have for hundreds of years used windmills. Today, some windmills are electric, and some have been replaced by electric pumps. With dikes, dams, windmills, and drainage systems of several kinds, the Dutch are always fighting the water.

Still, the water gives pleasure to most Dutch people, and some earn a living by it. When the canals freeze (usually only once in several years), Dutch adults and children skate on them. Fishing in this land of waterways is less important than you might think. But everyone looks forward to the herring caught in the spring.

There is some boating on the canals. But the Dutch do not go about the country mainly by water. The streets in Holland are full of people using buses, bicycles, and motorbikes.

H-4 Testing Yourself

Draw a line under each right answer or fill in each blank.

1. Although not stated in the article, you can tell that
   - a. Holland has no wind.
   - b. some people in Holland travel by water.
   - c. windmills are still in use in Holland.

2. This article as a whole is about
   - a. canals.
   - b. windmills.
   - c. Holland, a lowland country.
   - d. fishing in canals.

3. The word **them** in the third paragraph, second sentence, refers to

   _____.

4. Most windmills are run by electricity or gas.   Yes   No   Does not say

5. Which two of these sentences are not true?
   - a. The Dutch must always fight the water.
   - b. Holland is a high country.
   - c. Holland is near the sea.
   - d. Herring are caught in Holland.
   - e. Fishing is Holland's most important industry.

6. What word in the second paragraph, second sentence, means a **high bank built to**

   keep out water? _____

Getting Ready to Read

oyster
demand
material
dumped
increases
yearly
consume
planned
introduced
raised

Draw a line under each right answer or fill in the blank.

1. **Grown** means   **raised**   **demanded**   **consumed.**

2. **Grows larger** means   **dumps**   **plans**   **increases.**

3. **Brought into use** means   **demanded**   **introduced**   **planned.**

4. **Emptied out** may mean   **planned**   **demanded**   **dumped.**

5. **Each year** means   **oyster**   **yearly**   **material.**

6. It means **use up.** _____

H-5   Farming in the Ocean

Have you ever heard of a farm on the floor of the ocean? Sometimes, people are surprised to learn that such farms are common. They are oyster farms. The meat of the oyster is a very popular food in many countries of the world and in the United States as well.

Oysters are found in the ocean near the coastline. For a great many years, the supply of oysters was more than equal to the demand. However, the number of oysters from natural oyster beds is getting smaller. In part, this is because more waste material is dumped in oceans. Also, the demand for oysters increases yearly. This is true for two reasons. First, the population has grown. Second, many of us consume

more seafood than in the past.

Planned oyster farming was introduced to solve the problem. About 10,000 metric tons (11,000 tons) of oyster meat is raised yearly on oyster farms. It takes many oysters to make just one pound or kilogram. The raising of oysters on the floor of the ocean is a big farming industry.

H-5 Testing Yourself

NUMBER RIGHT

Draw a line under each right answer or fill in each blank.

1. Although not stated in the article, you can tell that
   - a. oyster farms must be careful about pollution.
   - b. oysters have a shell.
   - c. oyster farming is run by the government.

2. This article as a whole is about
   - a. wheat farming.
   - b. eating fish.
   - c. things people like to eat.
   - d. a kind of planned farming.

3. The word **they** in the third sentence refers to _____.

4. Oysters are sold by the pound or kilogram.   Yes   No   Does not say

5. Which two of these sentences are not true?
   - a. Waste is good for oyster farms.
   - b. Oyster farms are near the coast.
   - c. Oysters grow in the sea.
   - d. Oysters can be eaten.
   - e. Oysters are not often eaten in the United States.

6. What word in the first sentence of the last paragraph means **thought out in advance**? _____

Getting Ready to Read

SAY AND KNOW

glacier
iceberg
masses
layer
uneven
crevasses
compressed
firmly
eventually

Draw a line under each right answer or fill in the blank.

1. **Squeezed together** means   masses   layer   compressed.

2. **Not equal** may mean   firmly   uneven   iceberg.

3. **One thickness** is called a   crevass   mass   layer.

4. **The opposite of loosely** is   eventually   firmly   masses.

5. **A large mass of ice** is a   glacier   masses   layer.

6. **Deep cracks in a glacier** are called _____.

H-6   Rivers of Ice

A glacier is really a river of ice. The ice moves somewhat in the same way as water in a river does. The movement is very slow, however, and is seldom more than 24 inches (60 centimeters) a day. When the glacier reaches the ocean, pieces break off. These pieces are called icebergs.

Glaciers are formed when the amount of snow that falls during the year is more than the amount that melts. The masses of snow are compressed and slowly changed into ice. As new layers of ice are formed each

year, those on the bottom become more and more firmly packed down. Eventually the ice begins to move.

The ice moves more slowly at the sides and the bottom than it does at the top and center. This is because the ice at the sides and the bottom rubs against rock. The uneven movement causes the ice to crack. Huge openings called crevasses are formed. Some crevasses are more than 30 meters (100 feet) deep. Crossing a glacier is a very dangerous business.

H-6 Testing Yourself

NUMBER RIGHT

Draw a line under each right answer or fill in each blank.

1. Although not stated in the article, you can tell that

    a. icebergs have crevasses.   b. icebergs are small.

    c. usually the safest way to cross a glacier is by plane.

2. This article as a whole is about

    a. ice and snow.   c. crossing a glacier.

    b. crevasses.   d. glaciers and how they form and move.

3. The word **those** in the second paragraph, third sentence, refers to

    _____.

4. Crevasses sometimes close up.   Yes   No   Does not say

5. Which two of these sentences are not true?

    a. Glaciers are icebergs.   c. Glaciers are made of ice.

    b. Glaciers move quickly.   d. Icebergs are found in oceans.

    e. Glaciers usually move very little in a day.

6. What word in the last sentence means **going over?** _____

Getting Ready to Read

SAY AND KNOW

noting

position

sundials

cloudy

hourglass

announce

weights

accurately

windup

Draw a line under each right answer or fill in the blank.

1. **Place** means   **windup**   **noting**   **position.**

2. **Not clear** may mean   **cloudy**   **sundial**   **accurately.**

3. **To tell** is to   **announce**   **noting**   **windup.**

4. **In an exactly right way** means   **cloudy**   **weights**   **accurately.**

5. It **measures time.**   **windup**   **hourglass**   **weights**

6. Write the two words which make up the compound word **hourglass.**

_____ _____

H-7 Measuring Time

The sun served as the first clock. People guessed at the time of day by noting the position of the sun in the sky. Then they discovered that they could tell time by measuring the lengths of the shadows cast by a pole. Using this idea, they made and used sundials. These devices, however, did not work indoors, on cloudy days, or at night. People kept looking for better ways to measure time.

Candles marked with colored lines were used indoors. When a candle had burned from one colored line to the next, an hour had passed. Later water clocks of varying types and hourglasses were also used.

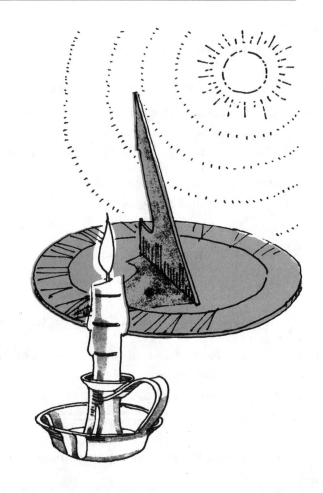

156

Finally, nearly 1000 years ago, the first clock was made. It had neither a face nor hands but had bells that rang each hour to announce the time. This clock and other early clocks were run by falling weights.

Today we can keep time accurately by using electric clocks and windup clocks run by springs. We also have battery-powered watches and clocks. Many show the time with numbers rather than by hands.

H-7 Testing Yourself

Draw a line under each right answer or fill in each blank.

1. Although not stated in the article, you can tell that

    a. water clocks were accurate.   b. the first clock was large.

        c. sundials were of little use at night.

2. This article as a whole is about

    a. hourglasses.   c. devices used to tell time.

    b. sundials.   d. the first clock.

3. The word **they** in the fourth sentence refers to _____.

4. Sundials were once used.   Yes   No   Does not say

5. Which two of these sentences are not true?

    a. The sun was the first clock.   c. Windup clocks are now used.

    b. Water clocks were once used.   d. Early clocks were electric.

        e. Candles were never used for anything but lights.

6. What word in the second sentence means **taking notice of?**

Getting Ready to Read

SAY AND KNOW

metropolitan
opera
rundown
projects
gospel music
conservatories
discouraged
motivated
ensure

Draw a line under each right answer or fill in the blank.

1. Which word means **in poor condition**? _____

2. **Things you set out to do** are   **dreams   operas   projects.**

3. It is sung in some churches. _____

4. **Schools where music is taught** are

                                                   conservatories   metropolitans   operas.

5. The opposite of **hopeful** is   **motivated   rundown   discouraged.**

6. **To make certain** is to _____.

H-8   Working for a Dream

Singing with the Metropolitan Opera Company in New York City must be every opera singer's dream. It is a dream that came true for Denyce Graves on October 7, 1995. Denyce's achievement was especially amazing.

Denyce grew up in a rundown neighborhood in Washington, DC. While Denyce's mother was at work, she expected Denyce and her sister and brother to do their homework, plus any additional projects she assigned them. The children were also expected to take care of household chores.

Denyce always loved to sing, but she knew nothing about opera. She sang gospel music at home and in the church choir. An elementary school teacher encouraged her to work on her singing. At Duke Ellington High School, she discovered opera.

After high school Denyce

studied music at the Oberlin and New England Conservatories. While in school, she worked at many jobs to support herself.

Success did not come easily. In fact, Denyce became so discouraged that she almost decided to stop singing. Then her big break came. The Houston Grand Opera Company asked her to be in their Young Artists Program. After that, she went on to sing with many other opera companies around the world.

What motivated Denyce? Here's how she put it: "Most of all, I wanted to realize my mother's belief that if you believe hard enough, work hard enough and take the right steps to ensure it, you can live the American Dream."

H-8 Testing Yourself

NUMBER RIGHT

Draw a line under each right answer or fill in each blank.

1. While not directly stated, it can be reasoned from the article that
   a. only the best opera singers get to sing with the Metropolitan Opera Company.
   b. Denyce hated school.
   c. Denyce's mother always wanted her to become a singer.

2. This article as a whole is about
   a. music education in America.   b. how Denyce Graves became an opera singer.
      c. Denyce Graves' childhood in Washington, DC.

3. The word **she** in the second sentence in paragraph two refers to

   _____.

4. Denyce has sung with the San Francisco Opera Company.   Yes   No   Does not say

5. Which two sentences are not true?
   a. Denyce's big break came in New York City.
   b. Denyce was an only child.
   c. Denyce studied at two different conservatories.
   d. Denyce almost gave up singing.
   e. As a child, Denyce sang in a church choir.

6. What word in paragraph two means **place where you live**?

   _____

Getting Ready to Read

Draw a line under each right answer or fill in the blank.

1. It means **stay.**   **deed**   **hoist**   **remain**

2. **Usual** means   **bitterly**   **express**   **ordinary.**

3. **Lift** means   **law**   **hoist**   **express.**

4. **Something done** is called a   **law**   **spare**   **deed.**

5. **A place where a person works** is called an   **office**   **express**   **elected.**

6. **Crying very unhappily** means **crying** _____.

H-9   Lincoln's Kind Deed

One morning, years before he was elected president, Abraham Lincoln was walking to his law office. He came upon a little girl standing beside a trunk in front of her house. She was crying bitterly. Lincoln stopped to ask what was the matter. The little girl told him that she was waiting for an express wagon to take her trunk to the train. She said that it was getting late and that if the wagon did not arrive soon she would miss the train and would have to remain at home.

"Oh, we will make the train," said Lincoln. "Just come with me."

He hoisted the trunk to his shoulder and started for the station. They arrived with no time to spare. The train had already arrived at the station. Lincoln put the little girl and her trunk onto the train. Then he went about his business as though he had done nothing out of the ordinary.

Abraham Lincoln was happy because he had helped someone. You may be sure that the girl never forgot his good turn.

H-9 Testing Yourself

Draw a line under each right answer or fill in each blank.

1. Although not stated in the article, you can tell that
   a. Lincoln once was a lawyer.   b. Lincoln was busy.
         c. the little girl was only 7 years old.

2. This article as a whole is about
   a. a kind deed.   c. a girl's trip.
   b. trains.   d. carrying a heavy trunk.

3. The word **she** in the third sentence refers to _____.

4. Lincoln lived in Ohio.   Yes   No   Does not say

5. Which two of these sentences are not true?
   a. Lincoln was kind.   c. Lincoln forgot the trunk.
   b. Lincoln was not helpful.   d. The express wagon was late.
         e. The child did not wish to miss her train.

6. What word in the third paragraph, second sentence, means **reached the desired place?** _____

A Contest between a Girl and a Crow

One day, Mother handed Lisa a half dollar. She told her to go to the store and buy a loaf of bread. Brighty, Lisa's pet crow, was fond of bright things. When it saw the half dollar, it flew after Lisa. She decided to tease the crow. She flipped the half dollar into the air. Each time Brighty saw the coin, the crow dashed for it.

Lisa flipped the half dollar higher and higher. Brighty darted for it and missed each time. The crow flew from one tree or fence post to another. It always kept its bright eyes on Lisa. She flipped the coin more often and higher. Then she flipped it once too often. This time when it came down, she couldn't catch it.

The coin spun along the side of the road. The crow grabbed for it. Away it flew, proudly clutching the prize. Lisa ran after it as fast as she could. Brighty flew on ahead and settled on the branch of a tree. The crow turned the shiny coin over and over with its claws and pecked at it. When Lisa came near, the crow held the coin with both claws, made a loud noise, and flew on.

Lisa saw no hope of getting the coin back. She was afraid the crow would lose it. Suddenly, she thought of trying to interest Brighty in something else. She found a bright stone and flipped it in the air. Brighty did not show much interest. Then Lisa held several bright things in her hand and spoke to the crow with kindness. But it flew away as soon as Lisa got close.

Lisa chased Brighty for a long time. Luckily, the crow kept flying

toward the village. When they were almost there, it settled on another post. This proved its undoing. Lisa came up with some bright things she had found. Among them was a piece of quartz. The quartz shone in the sun and caught Brighty's interest. The crow could not decide whether to trade the half dollar for this bright thing or to try to have them both. At last, Brighty let go of the half dollar. It dropped down into a hole in the top of the post.

Now the crow lost all interest in the shiny piece of quartz. It screamed and dug at the post with both claws.

Lisa rushed up. Brighty ruffled its feathers and pecked at the girl. Finally, she got the coin out of the hole. She ran to the village, bought the bread, and hurried home.

Adapted from "Youth's Companion"

MY READING TIME _____ (420 WORDS)

Thinking It Over

1. What are the two turning points in this story?

2. In this story, who was the more clever, the girl or the pet crow? Why?

3. Did Lisa deserve to get the money back, or did Brighty deserve to keep it? Why?

Getting Ready to Read

SAY AND KNOW

circular
cone-shaped
enemies
broad
losing
worry
expand
cling
nocturnal
retreat

Draw a line under each right answer or fill in the blank.

1. **Shaped like a circle** means   cone-shaped   circular   broad.

2. **The opposite of friends** is   losing   worry   enemies.

3. **To hang on** is to   retreat   expand   cling.

4. **To get bigger** is to   expand   circular   worry.

5. **The opposite of narrow** is   nocturnal   broad   expand.

6. It means **misplacing**. _____

I-1   With a Traveling House

The snail need never worry about losing its house, for this animal carries its house on its back. The house expands as the snail grows. Snail houses, or shells, may be of several different shapes. Circular shells and cone-shaped shells are common. A snail's shell protects it against most enemies. When the snail retreats into its shell, it is very hard to reach.

The snail has only one foot. It is almost as broad as the shell, and on this foot the snail can travel very safely. To make the foot cling to the surface on which the snail is moving, a sticky liquid is dropped from an opening just behind the animal's head. This sticky liquid also protects the snail from injury when it crawls across something sharp.

Snails are found in gardens and in damp places where there are well-watered plants for them to eat. Snails usually are nocturnal, but often they come out during or after a daytime rain.

I-1 Testing Yourself

Draw a line under each right answer or fill in each blank.

1. Although not stated in the article, you can tell that
       a. snails live underwater.   b. snails live in South America.
                 c. a snail has good natural protection.

2. This article as a whole is about
       a. the snail's food.   c. the snail.
       b. the snail's foot.   d. enemies of snails.

3. The word **it** in the first paragraph, last sentence, refers to _____.

4. Snails have two feet.   Yes   No   Does not say

5. Which two of these sentences are not true?
       a. Snails have shells.   c. Snails have no feet.
       b. Snails eat plants.   d. Snails live in damp places.
           e. Snails do not usually move about at night.

6. What word in the first sentence means **be troubled?** _____

Getting Ready to Read

SAY AND KNOW

monument
grave
beloved
owner
Buddhist
priest
remains
expensive
ceremonies
special

Draw a line under each right answer or fill in the blank.

1. **Parts that are left over** are   **beloved**   **remains**   **soul.**

2. **One who is loved** is   **beloved**   **grave**   **Buddhist.**

3. It means **costly.**   **ceremonies**   **special**   **expensive**

4. **Not ordinary** means   **remains**   **owner**   **special.**

5. **A place where a body is buried** is a   **grave**   **monument**   **priest.**

6. **Certain activities carried out at certain times** are called

     _____.

I-2   An Animal Cemetery

One of the unusual sights in Tokyo, the capital city of Japan, is a place where small animals are buried. Thousands of small marble monuments mark the graves of beloved animal pets. Under the monuments are buried goldfish, pigeons, rabbits, and birds, as well as cats and dogs.

Many of the graves are cared for by the people who once owned these animals. The other graves are maintained by the keepers of the animal cemetery. For a small

166

amount of money, the keepers of the cemetery will care for the grave of any small animal.

Near the animal cemetery stands a Buddhist temple. A Buddhist priest at the temple offers prayers for the souls of dead animals brought to the cemetery. After prayers have been said, the animal's body is burned. Then the remains are buried according to the wishes of the owner. Sometimes expensive ceremonies are held. Special graves are provided for animals whose owners wish to pay for them.

I-2 Testing Yourself

Draw a line under each right answer or fill in each blank.

1. Although not stated in the article, you can tell that
     a. many Japanese are fond of animals.   b. pets are large.
       c. there are many animal cemeteries in Japan.

2. This article as a whole is about
     a. a Buddhist temple.   c. a cemetery in Japan.
     b. small animal pets.   d. goldfish, pigeons, and rabbits.

3. The word **them** in the last sentence refers to _____.

4. There is an animal cemetery in Boston.   Yes   No   Does not say

5. Which two of these sentences are not true?
     a. People in Japan have no pets.   c. Animals may be buried.
     b. Some people have birds for pets.   d. Prayers may be said for pets.
       e. The graves are cared for free of charge.

6. What word in the second paragraph, second sentence, means **kept up?**

_____

Getting Ready to Read

SAY AND KNOW

queen
nursery
helpless
wiggle
lower
upper
transported
chambers
attendants
removed

Draw a line under each right answer or fill in the blank.

1. **A place for babies is a**   chambers   nursery   removed.

2. **To be taken is to be**   helpless   lower   transported.

3. **Unable to help oneself** means   queen   helpless   attendants.

4. **To move from side to side** is to   chambers   queen   wiggle.

5. It means **a set of rooms.**   chambers   lower   upper

6. It means **higher.** _____

I-3   Ant Nurses

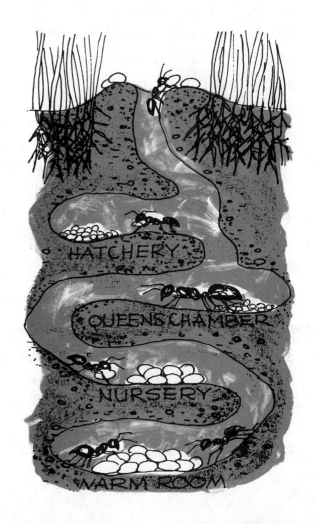

Ants have nurses for their babies just as some people have nurses for their children.

After the eggs are laid by the ant queen, they are picked up by the nurses and transported to another room. There they are watched until they hatch. At that time, they are removed to still another special room. This place is somewhat like a nursery.

When the ants are first hatched, they are very small and helpless. They can do nothing but wiggle about on the ground. The nurses must wash and feed them and keep them warm and safe. The nurses lick the babies to keep them clean and feed them several times a day. At night, they carry them down to the lower chambers where it is warm. In the morning, the nurses return the babies to the upper part of the nest. If the day is warm, the attendants may take them outside into the sunshine.

Baby ants need a great deal of care and attention. Some other baby insects and animals get this special kind of care, too.

I-3 Testing Yourself

Draw a line under each right answer or fill in each blank.

1. Although not stated in the article, you can tell that

    a. ants eat sugar.   b. the queen does not care for her babies.

        c. the ants' nurses are their mothers.

2. This article as a whole is about

    a. the queen ant.   c. an ant nest.

    b. caring for baby ants.   d. baby termites.

3. The word **they** in the second paragraph, second sentence, refers to

_____.

4. Ant nurses lay eggs.   Yes   No   Does not say

5. Which two of these sentences are not true?

    a. Ants hatch from eggs.   c. Ant babies sleep all the time.

    b. Ants live in groups.   d. The queen ant lays eggs.

        e. Ant babies care for themselves.

6. What word in the last paragraph, first sentence, means **special looking after?**

_____

Getting Ready to Read

SAY AND KNOW

located
northern
northeastern
southwest
composed
variations
variable
consistently
mostly
enormous
Labrador

Draw a line under each right answer or fill in the blank.

1. It means **very large.**   enormous   mostly   southwest

2. **Placed** means   northern   located   composed.

3. **Mainly** means   mostly   consistently   enormous.

4. **Changes** means   variable   variations   composed.

5. It is **the opposite of southern.**   northern   Labrador   northeastern

6. It means **made up.** _____

I-4   Facts about Labrador

Labrador is a large area located in the northeaster part of North America, southwest of Greenland. It has a seacoast over 700 miles (1120 kilometers) long. In spite of this, there are very few people living in Labrador. The country's population numbers only about 34,000. It is composed mostly of Inuits and other Native Americans.

In Labrador, the variations in temperature from summer to winter are enormous. Some days in summer are as warm as 90°F (34°C). This temperature is similar to that of our northern states in summer. In winter, however, Labrador is very cold, and temperatures some-

170

times fall as low as 45° below zero Celsius (about 50° below zero Fahrenheit). Because of the consistently variable climate, many of the native people change houses twice a year. These people live in houses of stone or wood in the winter and move to tents for the summer months.

The variations in temperature account for Labrador's small population. Such a climate discourages people who otherwise might settle there.

I-4 Testing Yourself

NUMBER RIGHT

Draw a line under each right answer or fill in each blank.

1. Although not stated in the article, you can tell that
   a. Labrador does not have large cities.   b. trees grow in Labrador.
   c. Labrador's population will probably never grow.

2. This article as a whole is about
   a. different temperatures.   c. living by the sea.
   b. a northern country.   d. tents and wood houses.

3. The word **it** in the second sentence refers to _____.

4. Labrador has warm winters.   Yes   No   Does not say

5. Which two of these sentences are not true?
   a. Eskimos live in Labrador.   c. Labrador has many people.
   b. Labrador is warm in summer.   d. Labrador is north of Greenland.
   e. Labrador's coast is over 700 miles long.

6. What word in the second paragraph, fifth sentence, means **weather?**

Getting Ready to Read

SAY AND KNOW

soybean
originally
Orient
recent
woody
enclosed
yield
processed
synthetic
versatile
tart

Draw a line under each right answer or fill in the blank.

1. **To give** means **to Orient yield woody.**

2. **Contained** means **enclosed processed recent.**

3. **Not long ago** means **tart soybean recent.**

4. **A manufactured substitute** is called **woody recent synthetic.**

5. **At first** means **processed versatile originally.**

6. It means **treated in a special way.** _____

I-5 A Versatile Plant

Soybeans were originally grown only in the countries of the Orient. In places such as China, Japan, and Korea, they are nearly as important a part of the diet as rice. Today, soybean crops are cultivated in the United States.

Soybeans, which sometimes grow over 2 meters (7 feet) tall, have thick, woody stems. The seeds are enclosed in pods. They grow easily in different types of soil. Soybeans yield a variety of useful products and have proved to be a valuable crop.

Soybean seeds contain a substance that can be processed and used as a milk substitute. Soybean oil can be used in making soap, synthetic rubber, paint, varnish, and margarine. Parts of soybeans can also be used to make meal, flour, and plastics. Some young soybeans can be canned or frozen and used for food. In addition, soy sauce, which is a tart sauce used to flavor food, is made from specially treated soybeans. As you can see, soybeans are unusually versatile plants!

I-5   Testing Yourself

Draw a line under each right answer or fill in each blank.

1. Although not stated in the article, you can tell that
    a. soybeans grow in Europe.   b. soybeans taste like milk.
        c. full-grown soybeans are not good to eat.

2. This article as a whole is about
    a. soybeans.   c. products.
    b. the Orient.   d. synthetic rubber.

3. The word **they** in the second sentence refers to _____.

4. Soybeans are small plants.   Yes   No   Does not say

5. Which two of these sentences are not true?
    a. Soybeans have many uses.   c. Soybeans were first found in the U.S.
    b. Soybeans have woody stems.   d. Soybeans grow only in sandy soil.
        e. Soybeans grow easily.

6. What word in the last sentence means **able to do or be different things.**

Getting Ready to Read

SAY AND KNOW

tusk
ivory
weapon
combat
allowed
male
female
illegal
international
ban

Draw a line under each right answer or fill in the blank.

1. **A thing used in fighting** is a   weapon   ban   combat.

2. **A boy or a man** is a   tusk   male   female.

3. **Something existing among nations** is called
       illegal   preserve   international.

4. **The opposite of forbidden** is   heavier   allowed   illegal.

5. **It means fighting.**   ban   weapon   combat

6. **The hard, white substance that makes up a tusk** is called

_____.

I-6   Valuable Teeth

Elephants are perhaps the only animals that have been hunted for their teeth. Elephants' tusks are the very large teeth growing on either side of their mouths. They are made of a material called ivory.

An elephant uses its long, pointed tusks as tools for digging in the ground for food. It also uses them as weapons in combat.

Male elephants' tusks are usually large and heavy. In Africa, female elephants have long, light tusks. In India and other parts of southern Asia, female elephants have small, short tusks or none at all.

Tusks in good condition are in great demand and may sell for

thousands of dollars. Because of this, large numbers of elephants have been killed. Some countries now try to protect elephants. These countries have established elephant preserves, or areas of land set aside for herds of elephants, where no one is allowed to harm them.

Most countries have now made the sale of ivory illegal. In addition, international laws ban the trade of ivory between countries.

I-6 Testing Yourself

NUMBER RIGHT

Draw a line under each right answer or fill in each blank.

1. Although not stated in the article, you can tell that
   a. elephants live in herds.   b. elephants live for many years.
       c. male elephants are hunted more.

2. This article as a whole is about
   a. elephants and their tusks.   c. African elephants.
   b. Indian elephants.   d. male elephants.

3. The word **their** in the first sentence refers to _____.

4. Ivory is very valuable.   Yes   No   Does not say

5. Which two of these sentences are not true?
   a. Male elephants have no tusks.   c. Tusks are made of skin.
   b. Indian elephants may have tusks.   d. Elephants dig for food.
       e. Each male elephant has two tusks.

6. What word in the fourth sentence of the fourth paragraph means **areas set up to**

   protect wildlife? _____

Getting Ready to Read

SAY AND KNOW	Draw a line under each right answer or fill in the blank.

SAY AND KNOW

diamond
score
simple
circumference
curved
diameter
certain
scholar
formula
wise

Draw a line under each right answer or fill in the blank.

1. **Easy** means **simple   score   circumference.**

2. **Not straight** means **diameter   wise   curved.**

3. **Sure** means **wise   certain   simple.**

4. It is **the name of a shape.   diameter   diamond   curved**

5. **A set method** is called **a   scholar   diameter   formula.**

6. **To gain points** sometimes means **to** _____.

I-7   Finding Distances

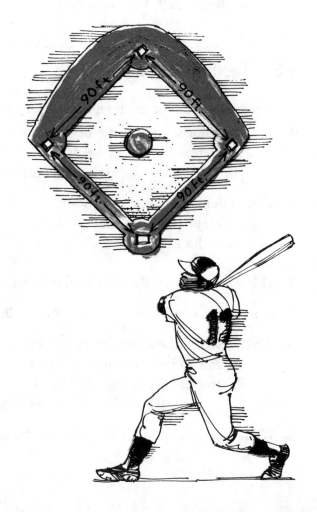

In order to score a run in baseball, a player must first hit the ball and then run all the way around the diamond. Each base must be touched in the run. Every standard baseball diamond is square in shape and measures about 90 feet (28 meters) on each side. Because there are four sides, you can measure the distance that a player must go to score a run by multiplying the length of one side by four.

It is not so simple to measure the circumference, or the distance around a circle. This is because the circumference is a curved line. However, you can measure across the center of a circle in a straight line. This straight line across the

176

center of a circle is called the *diameter*. Many years ago, a wise scholar devised a formula for finding the circumference of a circle. You will learn his formula later in your study of arithmetic. It involves multiplying the diameter of any given circle by a certain number. By multiplying the diameter of any circle by this number, you can find its circumference.

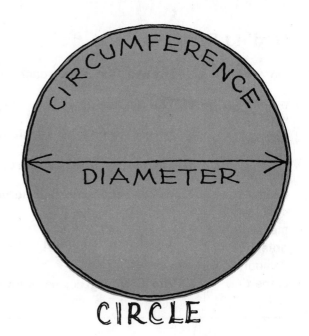

CIRCLE

I-7 Testing Yourself

NUMBER RIGHT

Draw a line under each right answer or fill in each blank.

1. Although not stated in the article, you can tell that
    a. diameters are curved.   b. baseball is popular.
    c. a player must run 360 feet to score a run.

2. This article as a whole is about
    a. playing baseball.   c. measuring distances.
    b. scoring a run.   d. measuring a circle.

3. The word **its** in the last sentence refers to _____.

4. Measuring circumference is very simple.   Yes   No   Does not say

5. Which two of these sentences are not true?
    a. A ball diamond is square.   c. We can measure curved lines.
    b. A ball diamond has five sides.   d. A diameter is a straight line.
    e. A ball diamond measures ninety meters on each side.

6. What word in the first sentence is the name of a **popular sport?**

Getting Ready to Read

Draw a line under each right answer or fill in the blank.

1. **The beginning is the   legend   emperor   origin.**

2. **An old story is a   Valentine   legend   message.**

3. **The end of life is   custom   marry   death.**

4. **Words sent from one person to another are a**

     married   prison   message.

5. **A jail is a   legend   prison   message.**

6. **Words that greet someone** are _____.

I-8   Valentine's Day

Several different stories are told about the origin of Valentine's Day. One legend dates as far back as the days of the Roman Empire. According to the story, Claudius, the Emperor of Rome, wanted to increase the size of his army. He knew that it would be easier to get young men who were not married to join. Therefore, he made a rule that no young man could marry until he had served a certain number of years in the army.

A priest named Valentine broke the rule. He performed secret marriages for a great many young people. Finally, Claudius found out about this and put the priest in

prison. Valentine remained there until his death on February 14.

After his death, Valentine was named a saint. The day of his death was named Saint Valentine's Day. It became the custom for lovers to send each other messages on this day. Now Valentine's Day is a time for people to send one another greetings of many kinds.

I-8 Testing Yourself

NUMBER RIGHT

Draw a line under each right answer or fill in each blank.

1. Although not stated in the article, you can tell that
   a. Claudius liked to fight.   b. Valentine was a young man.
      c. no one is sure about the origin of Valentine's Day.

2. This article as a whole is about
   a. a priest named Claudius.   c. the death of an emperor.
   b. a special day.   d. the Roman Empire.

3. The word **he** in the fourth sentence refers to _____.

4. Claudius died on February 14.   Yes   No   Does not say

5. Which two of these sentences are not true?
   a. Valentine was an emperor.   c. This story is a legend.
   b. Claudius married Valentine.   d. Greetings are sent on February 14.
               e. Claudius was Emperor of Rome.

6. What word in the third paragraph, third sentence, means a **common practice?**

Getting Ready to Read

SAY AND KNOW

statue

material

site

engineer

wharf

building

architect

publisher

Draw a line under each right answer or fill in the blank.

1. **A figure carved in stone or other hard material** is a

   site   statue   wharf.

2. **Someone who draws plans for a building** is

   an architect   a publisher   an engineer.

3. **The place where a building is to be** is a   site   statue   wharf.

4. **A place where boats can dock** is a   site   building   wharf.

5. **A person or company that prints and sells newspapers and maga-**

   zines is a _____.

I-9   The House that Julia Built

In California, there is a very unusual "ranch." It has a house with about 150 rooms, 31 bathrooms, and indoor and outdoor

swimming pools. It sits on hundreds of acres of ground. Animals used to roam freely through the grounds. The "ranch" is San Simeon Castle. The person in charge of building it was an architect named Julia Morgan.

A newspaper and magazine publisher, William Randolph Hearst, put up San Simeon. He spent time there riding and swimming. That may be one reason he called it a ranch. But in fact, this home was made from parts of many European castles. Towers, statues, even whole rooms were shipped from Europe to be used for building San Simeon.

Julia Morgan had to do more than plan how San Simeon would

look. She had to figure out how to get the heavy stone to the building site. But she was also an engineer. She knew how to solve such problems. The castle was to be on top of a hill above the sea. Morgan had a wharf built. Materials were brought to San Simeon by boat and unloaded at the wharf. Then they were hauled uphill.

Julia Morgan planned many other buildings, but San Simeon Castle is her most famous and unusual work.

I-9   Testing Yourself

Draw a line under each right answer or fill in each blank.

1. Although not stated in the article, you can tell that
   a. San Simeon Castle cost a lot of money.   b. Julia Morgan was an architect.
   c. Julia Morgan was very rich.

2. This article as a whole is about
   a. a woman architect's biggest job.   c. women who build houses.
   b. houses in California.   d. ranch houses.

3. The word **it** in the second sentence refers to _____.

4. The castle has indoor and outdoor pools.   Yes   No   Does not say

5. Which two of these sentences are not true?
   a. Julia Morgan was not an engineer.   c. Julia Morgan built a wharf.
   b. Julia Morgan built only one building.   d. Hearst liked to swim.
   e. Parts of the castle came from Europe.

6. What word in the third paragraph, second sentence, means **a spot where a building**

   is to be? _____

A Mighty Hunter

Once when I was near the bank of a large body of water in Sri Lanka, I thought I heard a rustling noise behind me. On facing about, I almost turned to stone at the sight of a lion. It appeared to be coming toward me with the intention of using me for a meal without my permission. What was to be done? My gun was loaded only with swan shot. I had no heavier lead with me. I could have no idea of killing such an animal with swan shot. Yet I had some hopes of frightening it by the sound. So I let fly without waiting until it was within reach. The noise only made the beast angry. It came at me full speed. I turned to escape and saw behind me a large crocodile with open jaws all ready to receive me. On my right was the large body of water.

On my left was a deep canyon. I gave myself up as lost. The angry lion was now on its hind legs ready to grab and claw me. Just as it leaped, I fell to the ground with fear. The lion sailed over me.

There I lay, expecting each moment to feel teeth and claws in some part of my person. Instead I heard a loud and very strange noise. It was different from any sound that I had ever heard before. Finally I raised my head. I looked about. To my great joy, I saw that the lion, in trying to have dinner upon me, had leaped over my body and into

the wide-open jaws of the crocodile! The head of the lion was stuck in the throat of the other beast. Each was trying very hard to be rid of the other. With my hunting knife, I cut off the lion's head at one blow. Then with the big end of my gun, I helped the lion's head farther into the throat of the crocodile. As it could neither swallow nor cough up this head, the crocodile died instantly.

At this moment of victory over two such powerful beasts, a friend arrived in search of me. I was patted on the back for my great victory. Then we measured the beast with the lion's head in its throat. It was 12½ meters (40 feet) in length. My friend was related to a high-ranking officer. I told the officer of this strange and dangerous adventure. At once a wagon and servants were sent to get the bodies of the two hapless beasts.

The lion's skin with its hair on was made into bags for holding tobacco. I presented these bags to the heads of cities when I returned

to Holland. In return, I was presented with a large sum of money as a fitting reward.

The skin of the crocodile was stuffed and mounted and was presented to the public museum at Amsterdam. The guide at the museum tells the whole story to each visitor with such changes as seem proper. Some of the changes that the guide makes from the real truth are rather surprising. So little feeling has this person for the truth that a good deal is often added to the real story as I have just told it to you.

Once I heard the guide tell a group of visitors that the lion had jumped clear through the crocodile from its jaws to the tip of its tail. Then, as the lion's head appeared on its hurried journey, the brave hunter had cut off the head of the lion and, at the same time, at least three sections of the other monster's tail! The guide did not stop here but went on to add ever more to the tale. As soon as the great crocodile

missed its tail, the beast grabbed the hunting knife from the hunter's hand. The crocodile's haste was so great, however, that it swallowed the knife and cut its own throat, dying instantly.

This lack of feeling for the truth on the part of the guide sometimes causes me to wonder if the truth of my own tale may be doubted.

Adapted from John Martin

MY READING TIME _____ **(700 WORDS)**

Thinking It Over

1. Do you think the teller of the story has much feeling for the truth?

2. What is it that makes this story humorous?

3. Does the storyteller expect the reader to believe this tale? How can you tell?

4. What is it about the way this story is told that makes it believable?

5. Why was the storyteller given the large sum of money?

Keeping Track of Growth

Study this sample graph. To record the score for Unit A, put a dot on the line beside the number which tells how often Question 4 was answered correctly. Do the same for Units B, C, and so on. Draw a line to join the dots. The line will show how this reading skill is growing.

Notice that each graph records the progress made on one question. See how this reader improved in answering Question 4 in each unit except Unit E.

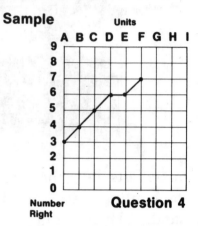

Sample

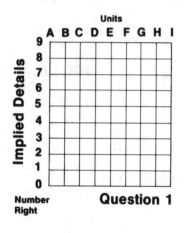

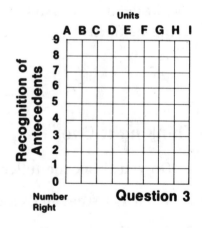

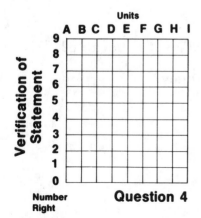

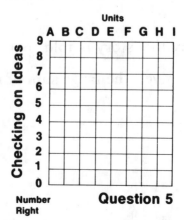

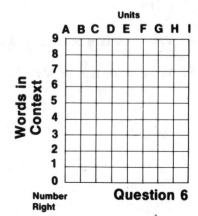